With L♡VE
from Bunty

a biography
by Jean Goodman

FRONT JACKET PAINTING
Message
Exhibited in the Royal Academy 1982

TITLE-PAGE
Self-portrait of the artist

WITH LOVE FROM BUNTY

Published by Parke Sutton Publishing Limited
The Old Tannery, Barrack Street, Norwich NR3 1TS

Text copyright © 1992 Jean Goodman
Designed by Gillian Matthews
This edition copyright © 1992 Parke Sutton Publishing Limited
Reprinted 1993
ISBN 1-870337-11-5

Printed in England by Thorndick and Dawson Limited

FOREWORD

Bunty Miller's long and successful career as a self-taught painter was enriched, (often it must be said at the expense of her painting), by her tireless capacity for friendship and her solicitude for others of all generations. But, like every true artist, she was aware of the particular danger in this. She knew that art can only flourish and grow in silent loneliness and self-obsession with the task in hand, but she could never resist dropping her brush to help somebody out with some temporary difficulty or with a new and imaginative enterprise.

Bunty was justly proud that her work was exhibited uninterruptedly for twenty-nine years in the Royal Academy's Summer Exhibition – which must surely be a record – and it must have been a continuing pleasure to know her paintings were in such constant demand.

Her favourite subjects were studies of still life.

'A bowl of flowers doesn't chatter,' she would say, 'and has no relations saying "It's lovely but there is something wrong with the jug handle".'

Nevertheless, she was also a skilful and busy portrait painter with a gift for catching a likeness. She accepted the discipline demanded of the portrait painter, where every subject is subtly different, and therefore often more challenging than her familiar still life studies.

To whatever she attempted she brought serious attention. Her eye was as pin-sharp as a poacher's and she excelled in depicting the miniature (note the terrifying tiny detail of the postage stamp in the picture *Parcel of Flowers*).

Bunty was beautiful and talented. She had a long, busy creative life, warmed by the company of her family and friends. She obviously enjoyed what she did so well, and now, through this book, we too can still share in that enjoyment in the company of her work.

SIR HUGH CASSON

To darling Bunt, with
all my love — Jimmy.

*B*unty Miller was born on 11th June, 1919 in Rhanikhet, one of the loveliest hill stations high in the Himalayas. She was born in her grandparents' house which overlooked a breath-taking panorama of snow-capped mountains stretching for miles beyond the pine forests where black bear, leopard, tiger and panther roamed.

Her mother, like most Indian Army officer's wives, had gone to the hills to escape from the intense heat before the monsoon. The glittering setting embodied the colourful traditions of the Raj which was Bunty's legacy and dominated the first thirty years of her life.

Both painting and a military tradition were in her blood. Her father, Captain Guy Pearson of the 53rd Sikh's Frontier Force, served in India and became A.D.C. to his father, General Sir Alfred Pearson, K.C.I.E. Her maternal great-grandfather was Ayrton Pullan, an army colonel and a keen and accomplished landscape artist, from whom Bunty apparently inherited her artistic talent.

It came down to her through his daughter, Bunty's grandmother, who was a skilful water-colourist. Her ability to draw was passed to her daughter, Enid, as evidenced by the brilliant line drawings that spattered the pages of her letters. However, Enid Pearson, Bunty's beautiful and accomplished mother, had too many distractions to spend time developing her artistic streak.

She was the most important influence in Bunty's life. Warm and loving, generous and imaginative, she subjugated her undoubted acting ability and her longing for a stage career to the role of a devoted army wife. In 1915, as a newly-engaged twenty-year-old, she wrote to her soldier fiancé:

The evacuation of Warsaw is bad news, isn't it darling? Do you think any native troops will be sent to Russia to help when the combined attack comes? Your Mother confessed to me she hoped you wouldn't be sent off. I felt there was someone as wicked as me in the world.

As a matter of fact I do want you to go as I know how you pine to and what a difference it would make to you afterwards and, of course, we would both gladly go through anxious times feeling you were getting your just chance and you would do splendidly.

During their three-year engagement

Enid Pearson
The devoted mother from whom Bunty inherited a great capacity to give and receive love, a lack of inhibition and her artistic talent.
Watercolour 1951.

5

she wrote to him daily, sometimes twice a day, whenever they were apart. Her loving and caring letters, amazingly frank and outspoken for their time, portrayed a vivid picture of the privileged domestic life of the Raj. Her days were packed with riding, swimming, tennis, parties, balls and shoots, amateur theatricals and vice-regal ceremonies.

Romance and flirtations were rife in a cultureless society centred round that unique British institution, the local Club. Enid, glamorous and affectionate with, according to an old friend, 'an aura of happiness and charm that always attracted a circle of admirers', found that her engagement ring was no deterrent to other suitors, much to the anxiety of Guy.

One of the many entries from Bunty Miller's Common place Book, where she expressed her feelings in favourite quotations and original writings.

MOTHERS.

Mine the BEST, most sublime, SELFLESS, warm, loving, cheerful, enthusiastic, appreciative, talented, positive, funny, dog-doting, SHARING, BEAUTIFUL, tender beyond words, so CARING, passionate flow a lova, a great talent for words & language - a marvellous letter writer & FRIEND - a brilliant actress - the career she gave up for us 3 daughters.

He was reassured to learn she was diligently acquiring domestic skills such as, 'the dhobie should iron the table-cloth on the table before dinner so you don't get the folding up creases'.

She also had a fine sense of the dramatic and a very determined streak:

... those shreds of torn-up letter in the fireplace were not written by the Guy I love, she wrote, *but by a very seedy and depressed edition of him so I shall not refer to it again, only he forgot that he has no right to be as authoritative as that to anyone but an owl or a mouse and your sweetheart is neither.*

Dearest, let us mutually forgive each other and consider that our first quarrel has been got through and merely strengthened our love. We must sometimes have them to test it and, of course, it would be quite dull if we always agreed.

They were married in 1916. Their first child was born three years later and was christened Suzanne but nicknamed herself Bunty as soon as she could talk. Pamela was born three years after, followed, seven years later, by Fay. They made a glamorous trio as each was beautiful in her own way. However, Bunty in particular had inherited her mother's love of beauty, her lack of inhibition and her great capacity to receive and express love – in words and deeds, along with generations of artistic ability.

Like most children whose parents served in India, Bunty and Pamela were sent to boarding school in England. In 1932 they went to Wadhurst College, a newly-established independent school for girls set in sixty-five acres of Sussex countryside, near Tunbridge Wells.

Bunty hated it but, from her first day there, she proved as enthusiastic a correspondent as her mother, and her letters spilled over with an affection that almost masked the homesickness. It was the start of a lifelong habit of writing warm caring letters to her mother whenever they were apart for even a few days. The affection and intimacy between mother and daughter was remarkable.

My Darling and own Mum, read her first letter, *We are only allowed quarter of an hour to write in. I think it is <u>wicked</u> don't you. Oh! Mum I hope you won't get worried will you darling ... Oh! dear if we only had time to write lovely long letters to you like you do to us. DO send me a photo of you. I <u>do</u> so need one so badly mum darling ... We are longing to hear home news as it is more interesting than anything else.*

A week later she wrote:

When you come to say Goodnight to me in my imagination and when you give me a little hug and tell us a little story I <u>simply</u> long for you darling and so then I write a letter to you and it comforts me most <u>awfully.</u> It seems as though I am talking to you sweet mum. We are very lucky really to have you and dad.

I drew and painted a picture of my own idea and I got Very Good written on

Cornucopia
Oil on canvas 1956.

the back. It has been nailed up in our classroom and everybody admires it, also another one I drew and painted of the 'Tempest' at moonlight for Miss Mulliner has been put up in the middle school classroom, they think I am a very good drawer, Mum darling, I am glad they think that, because I am such a dreadful dunce at everything else.

It seemed that nothing else in the school's full curriculum interested her. She found arithmetic 'quite impossible' and resented the discipline so much that, with an older girl, she tried to escape from a dormitory window at night. They were caught, fully clothed under the bed-covers by a mistress before the adventure had even started, which was perhaps fortunate as the window was a good twenty feet above the ground.

Vacations were spent in an easy-going holiday home, Oaklands at Maidenhead run by a Mr and Mrs Ogden, for boys and girls whose parents were abroad. Bunty loved the happy-go-lucky atmosphere, the summer seaside picnics and camping trips and the winter shopping expeditions to London with visits to museums, art galleries and theatres. Eventually, the Ogdens decided to turn their home into a boarding school for girls aged ten to sixteen, and Bunty and Pamela persuaded their parents to let them go there. Bunty left Wadhurst College thankfully and with the one distinction of having gained the

Royal Art Society's six diplomas by the age of fifteen.

Oaklands school, staffed by only two teachers and a young French student was much more to her liking. According to her best friend, Jemima Hollins, (later Jemima King-Martin), Bunty never did any work.

'She'd say, "What's prep tonight?" and I'd say, "Reading" and she'd say, "Oh good! Nothing to do!" Often I'd précis it for her.

'She was extremely idle and didn't seem to have much energy. [Possibly the start of the thyroid trouble that persisted throughout her life.] She was always drawing but never seemed to finish anything. I used to say, "Look here. You haven't got anything else except your face so you must stick to your drawing and painting."

'She was such a mixture of irresponsibility and dedication to her art. But she was so gorgeous to look at that all the boys were completely smitten and offered her constant distractions which made it extra hard for her to stick to drawing and painting.'

Enid Pearson visited her daughters in their second year at school and decided that, for Bunty at any rate, it was a complete waste of time. She was sent to a Swiss finishing school, La Printinière at Arvés-Villars run by 'Tante Galle', a lady whom everyone adored. Bunty stayed for two years and was in her element. A letter home mentioned a young Italian Count who hoped to become a diplomat and of whom she had grown 'awfully fond'. She was sure her parents would like him tremendously.

Only French was spoken in the school. In winter, Bunty made brave attempts to ski and in summer she swam and played tennis, but was happiest roaming the mountainside for wild flowers to paint and press. Each week she had an hour's private drawing lesson from a M. Schimek and longed to go every day. She drew portraits of her friends and tried her hand at oil-painting.

She also spent many hours studying a present of an album of the works of great artists. Like many teenagers she was completely captivated by Vermeer's *Head of a Young Girl* portraying a mood of dreaming anticipation that mirrored her own. The textured cream dress and blue silk turban, illustrating the subtle effect of light on colour, may have made a lasting impression on a girl for whom the play of light on inanimate objects and their texture would become a major feature of her own painting.

By then, although drawing and painting were Bunty's chief pastimes, there were no signs they were a driving ambition. Life was for fun and excitement and romance, and the prospect of the glittering social whirl in the pre-war élite of England or India offered an irresistible attraction.

The débutante as presented at court in 1937.

She was seventeen-and-a-half when her mother presented her at Court. Serenity and mischief can be detected in the photograph of the beautiful débutante in her obligatory white gown.

Two weeks after her eighteenth birthday she went to a Royal garden party at Buckingham Palace. After that one glimpse of the London season, Cinderella-like she was on a slow boat to India to join her parents at Rourkee where her father was the Lieutenant Colonel in command of his regiment.

Bunty was immediately lionised by a bevy of young officers, and drawing was relegated to sketching designs for the clothes she needed for a diary full of invitations. Within months of her arrival, however, her parents' pride in her success was tempered with misgiving when she became engaged to Hugh Hill, a tall, dark officer in the Ghurkas.

They made a spectacular-looking couple and, for two years, Bunty appeared to be idyllically in love. But by 1939 there was still no talk of marriage, ostensibly because of the imminence of war. Although Hugh was often away on duty, life was sweet for Bunty, living with her parents and with no shortage of escorts waiting to substitute for Hugh. She was happy and radiant, an incorrigible romantic in love with love.

On a visit to the hill station at Mount Abu with her father, then Military Adviser to the Jaipur State Forces, she went with a party of young people to a ball. At midnight, a handsome young subaltern asked her to dance. He was James Miller, on leave from his regiment on the North West Frontier, and was staying with his sister nearby.

'Bunty looked simply wonderful,' he recalled. 'She was so much in demand that I decided not to ask her to dance until midnight. Then it was quite unbelievable. We danced until the band went home and then I took her back to the Residency. I had got a lift to the dance so had no car there and we walked home through jungle-infested country. Bunty was terrified because she knew there were panther around. There

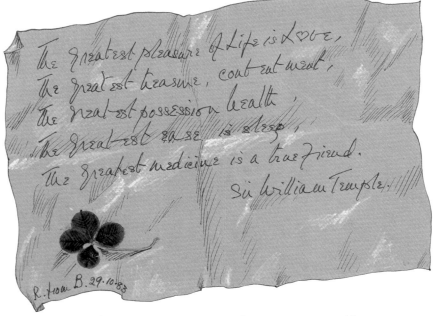

The greatest pleasure of Life is Love,
The greatest treasure, contentment,
The greatest possession, health,
The greatest ease is sleep,
The greatest medicine is a true friend.

Sir William Temple.

R. from B. 29.10.83

was a full moon and we talked in the Residency's gorgeous garden until dawn. That was the start of our lifetime's incredible romance.'

Their romance, however, would always be punctuated by advances from other men who found Bunty's amazing looks irresistible. One month after she met Jimmy, Hugh's engagement ring arrived.

It's so lovely, she wrote to her mother. *But I do so wish I'd had it ages ago or not at all. The shock of realising I wasn't thrilled to get it horrified me. (I am <u>vile</u>.)*

She took the ring with her when she visited her old school friend Jemima to think things over. Jemima was living with her father, the Director General of Police in the United Provinces. From there Bunty wrote to her mother:

There are ten regiments here and only three other girls beside Jemima and me and they don't look like anything. This place is one party after another and dances and moonlight sailing etc. etc. It's really quite incredible. Rather fun for a bit.

Darlingest Mum. Coming home from the dance last Saturday Bobbie proposed to me and told me that as he's eleven years older than me, he can look after me as I need and that I would make him terribly happy and he's completely in love with me and he said he could give me nearly everything I wanted.

It's no use choosing a man who needs cossetting, reassurance, a manic worrier who wants a domestic psychiatrist to boost his ego, because a man like that is a Life's Dedication in himself.

Major James Miller ('Jimmy') at the start of his civilian career.

Why is it darling that the wrong people are the right age and have money? He's very nice and amusing and a very good dancer and he's lucky enough to have heaps of money. He has plenty of savoir faire – always says the right thing and notices clothes and things and is a very good polo player. But, somehow darling, he's not artistic and he's a snob and we've not much in common although he always makes one feel at one's best.

In fact it's Jimmy I'm in love with so that's that. But it's fun to be taken around in Bobbie's sports car from polo to dances and seeing him order bottles of champagne and offering people cigarettes from the most superb case you've ever seen.

You see all that just appeals to the Material side of me which isn't good – but you can see how entertaining it could be.

Other officers took her flying and taught her to sail.

We've sailed by moonlight twice, she wrote. *It was absolutely heaven. I've never seen anything so romantic and beautiful.*

Despite social and romantic distractions, Bunty came to her decision and, at the end of her visit, returned Hugh's ring. A month later, in August 1940, she announced her engagement to Jimmy Miller. He was the son of an officer in the Indian Forest Service who had died when Jimmy was ten.

Hugh Hill was hurt and angry by their broken engagement. He challenged his successor to a fight that never materialised and threatened to disrupt the wedding. But, eventually, he came to terms with his grief and kept in touch with Bunty for the rest of his life.

For Bunty an imminent war was no longer a deterrent to marriage as a stream of glowing letters to her mother showed:

Jimmy and I, after a <u>lot</u> of discussion and reading and talking with other people, have decided we want a jungle-camp shooting honeymoon. We're <u>thrilled</u> darlings – and <u>after all</u> I shall be able to shoot 'my' panther !!! J is finding out about jungles which are cold enough for fires at night and we've heard first hand that the Sanfor jungles are full of panther and peacocks.

They were married in Jaipur on 2nd November, 1940, with a reception in the grounds of her parents' bungalow attended by many distinguished military and diplomatic guests. They included two sons of the Maharajah of Jaipur, who lent the newly-weds his lakeside lodge for the start of their honeymoon. Afterwards, they drove to a shooting lodge in the Central Province kept for the use of the Viceroy of India.

The lodge was beside a duck-covered lake where, with midnight visits from tiger and panther, Jimmy had all the shooting he wanted while Bunty remained an admiring spectator, often from high in a tree.

They returned to Delhi to start married life in a home which consisted of two large tents with smaller tents for their bathroom and their four Indian servants. From then on they moved to other army tents or bungalows, wherever Jimmy was posted.

Bunty wrote to her parents at least once a week, and started her life-long habit of drawing full-size pins and threaded needles in the margins of her letters, as if to secure the pages. She dotted her 'i's' with little red hearts and painted ribbon bows on the backs of the

The Girl in the Green Scarf
Exhibited at the Royal Society of Portrait Painters in 1961 and in their exhibition that toured England.
Also at the Paris Salon.
Oil on canvas.

envelopes as if to tie them. These touches of *trompe l'œil* became her trademark and made her letters collectors' pieces among some of her friends.

As well as the scraps of paper, she sent them favourite quotations in her own distinctive handwriting – like those in her beloved common place book.

She revelled in the non-stop social life as her mother and grandmother had before her. Like the other officers' wives, she wore beautiful gowns copied from Chanel, Schiaparelli and other *haute couture* designers, made up by local dressmakers immediately the sketches and photographs of the originals arrived from England.

She had plenty of time to try her hand at pastel portraits. The likenesses she achieved were startling. She also tasted commercial success when her fashion sketches were bought by an English publication for the British called *The Onlooker,* rather like the English *Tatler.*

However, after a year of marriage, her modest professional career was interrupted by the birth of their daughter in Peshawar. Jimmy's regiment was on the road to Afghanistan preparing defences against the Russians and, afterwards, he would constantly be on the move as forces gathered to go to Burma. Bunty and their daughter, romantically named Undine after the allegorical water sprite who must marry a mortal and bear him a child in order to gain her soul, joined him whenever they could arrange to spend a few days together. Otherwise, Bunty and Undine lived in Simla with her parents.

Jimmy and Bunty made a glamorous couple – never more so than on the night when they attended a military ball. For some days the Shikari

Still Life for Venus
Exhibited at the Royal
Scottish Academy 1952.
Oil on panel.

Undine
Aged 14.
Oil on canvas.

(gamekeeper) had been telling them about a panther who had been seen roaming the neighbourhood. Jimmy was keen to get a shot at the animal and,

learning the Shikari had seen it near their bungalow earlier in the day, had taken his rifle with him to the ball.

The Shikari sat next to their driver in the front of their car. Suddenly, the car stopped. A panther was sitting in the road in their path, its golden eyes glistening in the headlights until it turned and jumped over a low wall into the forest.

Jimmy and the Shikari were after it in a flash and Jimmy killed it with his first shot. They then lifted it into the back of the car and Bunty daintily raised the skirts of her white chiffon dress to make room for it. She and Jimmy continued their journey with their feet on their warm footrest and, when they arrived at the dance, it was carried into the ballroom as a tangible excuse for their lateness.

'It was probably the first time a warm panther's been seen on a dance floor,' Jimmy said.

After a few days' holiday together, Jimmy and Bunty simultaneously developed malaria. Jimmy had it mildly but Bunty was desperately ill, aggravated by the fact that she was again pregnant. Colin was born in October 1943, while Jimmy was in Burma as Liaison Officer to General Slim, and he did not learn of his son's birth for six weeks, nor see him until he was nine months old. By then, Bunty had romantically named him Colin after the elfin boy who played the flute in one of her favourite books, *The Secret Garden*.

When Colin was eighteen months old he caught infantile paralysis and nearly died. He had almost recovered when Jimmy returned from Burma to carry out combined operations near Bombay. Later, he went to the Staff College at Quetta, joined a newly-formed regiment as second in command and, for the next three years, he was able to live with Bunty and the children. However, Bunty still found she had no time for painting much and she often longed to set up her easel.

She again consoled herself in her album of great painters. It became her first text book, and the old masters, including Titian, Velasquez and Fantin-Latour, were her first tutors. Eventually she compiled a picture-postcard album of the paintings that impressed her most and commented on them in the margins.

Initially, portraits were her main interest: Rembrandt's study of his old mother was, she wrote, *the most moving portrait of old age, quite apart from its brilliance.* Samuel Palmer's self-portrait from the Ashmolean Museum in Oxford was, she decided from a postcard, *surely one of the greatest self-portraits ever?* She was completely fascinated by the eyes in Van Dyck's study of Cornelius van der Geest from the National Gallery. *The eyes are magnificent*, she wrote, *they look wet and glistening, and one literally expects them to blink.* She had the gift

of a photographic memory, like many fine painters, and those eyes made an indelible impression.

Her ability for total visual recall

The Earl Peel
Oil on canvas 1950.

Red Taffeta Rose
Exhibited at the Royal Academy in 1959. This painting set the pattern for a lifetime of public acclaim. Reproduced by the Medici Society.
Oil on panel.

enabled her to absorb details from those paintings so that one day, when she had mastered the techniques behind them, they could often be specifically identified in her own work. For instance, an early love was for Ruben's portrait of a lady in *The Straw Hat*. She noted *the MASTERLY brush strokes in the ostrich feathers round the brim of the hat.*

Eventually, a swirl of just such ostrich feathers would be the main feature of a painting of her own in the Royal Academy.

Meanwhile, as she deliberately absorbed details of the pictures she probably, perhaps sub-consciously, assimilated some aspects of the techniques and composition as guide-lines for a half-dreamed of career.

In February 1947, Jimmy had his first home leave for eleven years. They rented a large house on the cliffs in the Cornish fishing village of Cadgwith and shared it with Bunty's sister, Pamela, and her two small children Adrian and Angela and two army families also on leave from India. It was a well-contrived arrangement in the post-war days of rationing because a household of fourteen qualified for a catering licence which meant few food shortages.

It was a wonderful summer. It seemed as if the sun shone every day and Bunty felt more energetic than at any time in her married life. The urge to paint was

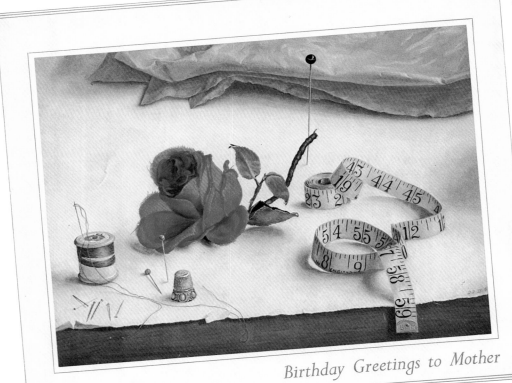

Birthday Greetings to Mother

insistent but, with no studio and no settled future, she could not think seriously about art.

Jimmy had missed England more than he realised and, by the autumn in that year of India's independence, he decided to retire from the army, with the rank of major, and look for a job where he could have a settled life with his wife and children. They had had more than thirty homes during their seven years of married life, and he felt it was time to put down roots and give Bunty her chance to paint. However, so many soldiers were coming out of the army that it was not easy to find a job. Eventually, they decided that while he was looking for one, Bunty and the children should pay a prolonged visit to her parents in Cyprus, to where Guy Pearson had retired a year previously with the rank of brigadier.

After several months Jimmy became a Guinness representative, based in Liverpool, and Bunty and the children sailed to join him. They spent Christmas 1947 aboard *S.S. Orbita*.

As usual, Bunty was very sea-sick for most of the time but, whenever she left her cabin, her beauty gave rise to problems.

In a letter to her parents from the ship she complained:

Two Polish officers are being rather tiresome, giving the children quantities of sweets, oranges, apples, chewing gum and making a terrific fuss of them,

Colin
Aged 10.
Oil on canvas.

sending me in caviar by them which I've made them take back three times – much as I'm tempted to eat it.

The ship's captain, it seemed, proved equally smitten and promised Undine he would give her his cap if she could persuade her mother to go ashore and have dinner with him when they docked at Gibraltar. It was the six-year-old daughter's earliest memory of a lifetime spent watching the inevitable attraction that her beautiful mother had for men.

'I remember being rather upset and revolted by the Captain's suggestion,' she said years later. 'All my life, I saw that men admired her and found her attractive. Apart from her looks she was such wonderful company and had the capacity to listen and take in everything people said, which made her very popular.'

All her life, Bunty had to cope with the burden of outstanding beauty. Flirting with men, perhaps, became her automatic response to their inevitable admiration. Both close friends and comparative strangers often tried to seduce her, but she learnt to deal with them promptly and effectively. Women also admired her beauty but were never jealous.

Undine, in her schooldays was 'terribly proud' of Bunty's blonde beauty.

'I always looked forward to sports' days and parents' days because she looked so ravishing,' she recalled. 'As I grew older, I always chose what she wore for those occasions, and made sure that she looked absolutely at her best.'

It must have taken considerable resourcefulness for Bunty to look her best in post-war England where she and Jimmy faced a dramatic reduction in their standard of living. At first, they flat-hunted from a small hotel in new Brighton and, eventually, found a four-roomed unfurnished flat in Blundell-sands, near Liverpool to rent for £5 a week. It left them £7 a week to live on after they had paid income tax and insurance.

Suddenly Bunty, to whom mathematics and money had always been enigmas, equated insurance with a new-found sense of responsibility. Her parents had promised her an allowance of £4 a month and, in a fulsome letter of thanks, she told them:

I've arranged to spend it all on insurance for the children. With the insurance we already have, they will get £500 each when they're 18, bless them!

She added that she had made long journeys into Liverpool or Southport every day to look for furniture and compare prices, while the children were left in the care of the hotel manager's daughter. She had also been to the Food Office three times for their ration books; to the Board of Trade for clothing coupons; arranged for the telephone to be installed; bought an electric cooker and measured their flat for curtains and floor covering.

Hard work but such JOY!!! she wrote, thrilled to have a home of her own at last.

She described a 'divinely comfy' secondhand sofa they had bought, with two chairs, for £124. They much preferred it, she wrote, *to cement-hard utility ones, roughly child's size, at £70 or non-utility at £200 which were MONSTERS of modernity and colouring.*

If ever any beauty I did see
Which I desired and got
'Twas but a dream of thee.

John Donne.

We went into it in a very big way, she assured them.

She proved a born home-maker. She described how she had fringed the ink-blue sofa in white to tie in with the curtain design of 'awfully pretty seagulls swooping and hovering'. They had just enough money left over to buy an asbestos-topped dining table, four chairs and three beds.

The Brigadier's daughter who, like her mother and grandmother before her, had always been cocooned in domestic luxury in India and had only to signal to one of her servants to do her bidding, approached her new life-style with an unexpected down-to-earth realism – much to her devoted husband's pride and amazement.

She made a first and last attempt to come to grips with money matters:

This week I'm writing down every penny I spend on food, she wrote to her parents. *... rations, fruit, veges, bread, milk and at the off-point store, and fish and Horlicks and so on. Then there's electric light, coal and wood, telephone and school fees (fairly small so far at £10 a term).*

Irene comes to clean two afternoons a week for 18s [90p] and there's our flicks and meals out. I don't think we'll be able to have Irene much longer.

Until then the kitchen had been virtually uncharted territory for Bunty, and she had rarely done so much as boil an egg. But she set to with a will and reported with pride:

On Sunday, I made a really rather super apple tart. We had roast beef, new potatoes and gravy and a steamed savoy cabbage. J and the children were so sweet and appreciative.

'I wish you were my doxy' said *The Earl of Lonsdale.*
Oil on canvas.

Her mother-in-law also made a brave show of appreciation when she paid them her first visit. Her inaugural meal, on the asbestos-topped table, was cauliflower *au gratin*. She cleared her plate and valiantly accepted a second helping. There were no complaints – although it transpired that Bunty had mixed all the ingredients for the cheese sauce and then failed to cook it before pouring it over the cauliflower.

In the novelty and ceaseless demands of her new life, Bunty had no time to unpack her paints and brushes. For the time being, she was too busy to feel a lack of fulfilment that Jimmy had begun to recognise in India.

Irene the cleaner stayed on. Her capacity for knitting sweaters for the children was discovered.

It's amazing that she can do one in a week as well as all her work. (Working class English women are as strong as horses), Bunty commented in a letter – perhaps enviously – at a time when painting meant staining and varnishing the drawing-room floor.

For eighteen months she fulfilled the unfamiliar role of a diligent housewife and devoted herself entirely to her husband and children. Their flat was too small for entertaining, they made no friends and their social life was restricted to visits to the theatre or cinema in Liverpool. Yet, according to her letters to her parents, she revelled in her new responsibilities.

Had a hell of a day yesterday doing the washing and starching J's collars, but I love ironing. I darn the children's socks <u>nearly every</u> day but I <u>love it</u>.

I really am a more useful person now.

Adrian Sykes
Aged 16.
Oil on canvas.

I used to be such a terrible SLOTH. And I'm getting more organised and efficient. It's extraordinary what necessity will do!!! I've got to the stage now where I wonder what on earth all one's servants

DID in India!!! (But it was very nice whatever it was!!!)

Suddenly, it all changed. Their life-style took a decided turn for the better in 1950 when Jimmy was upgraded and

'Note the terrifying detail of the postage stamp in *Parcel of Flowers*' – Sir Hugh Casson. Exhibited at the Royal Academy 1969.
Oil on panel.

appointed to represent Guinness in an area from Liverpool to Scotland. They rented a part-furnished beautiful nineteenth-century greystone house in the heart of the Lake District. The view was magnificent, and everything looked encouraging for a determined thirty-year-old housewife with a devoted husband. Finally, with virtually no art training, she resolved to become a professional painter.

The atmosphere of their new home, Hyning, near Kendal could not have been more conducive. It was an idyllic setting. Its garden was enclosed by low drystone walls, and it overlooked clusters of old cottages nestling in the folds of the rolling hills that stretched over to and beyond the shimmering waters of Morecambe Bay. It was a mile away from the stately Levens Hall, owned by Robin Bagot, a home which had been shrouded in legend and mystery since the thirteenth century.

Stories and legends abounded in the elegant little Hall where Bunty and Jimmy were frequent visitors. For the first time, the would-be painter found herself in an English family home where priceless treasures were the background to everyday life. Bunty, the romantic, could only have had her imagination fired by the combination of beauty and legend around her.

In the small panelled drawing-room, there was a magnificent carved overmantle, portrayed in the *Encyclopaedia Britannica,* and an exquisite Sèvres coffee service brought from France by the Duke of Wellington after Waterloo for his niece, Robin Bagot's great-grandmother. Bunty perhaps fingered a quilt of the oldest known patchwork, similar in design to the plasterwork of the ceiling in St James's Palace, and made by an owner of the house in 1708. Its thirty-two stitches to the inch must have been worked by a needlewoman who, like Bunty, had a 'watch-maker's eye'. Jimmy probably could not have resisted handling the seventeenth-century pair of pistols – the oldest in England.

Most important for Bunty, a wealth of fine paintings ensured that art was a main topic. There were early Florentine and Flemish pictures, De Wint watercolours, oils by Cotman and Constable and several Dutch works including a magnificent version of *The Holy Family* by Pieter Koeck van Aelst. Most intriguing of all, was a portrait of Anne of Hungary by Rubens which was a copy of the original by Mahler. It was a rare instance of a copy being more valuable than the original.

'I persuaded her that Rubens was a God,' Robin Bagot recalled with satisfaction.

He was a born teacher and Bunty was

LOVE

Love may really be more a capacity for love in oneself than anything very lovable in the person concerned.

in her element. There were dinner parties in a dining-room whose walls were covered with seventeenth-century tooled Cordova leather, and where the long refectory table gleamed with fine porcelain and old silver. Bunty bought silver slippers for a ball to wear with a borrowed white lace gown lined with sweet-pea coloured silk. The talk was always witty and wide-ranging and

Red Silk Shoes
Exhibited at the Royal Academy 1962. Reproduced by the Medici Society. Oil on panel.

Bunty, 'very lovely and amusing and with quite a dirty mind,' according to her many-talented host, was a great asset.

Robin Bagot was a wise art collector and a very able painter who had been taught by his father, a water-colourist and a pupil of Burne Jones. He was also an amateur astronomer, a musician who made as well as played the harpsichord and an amateur magician. While a prisoner of war in Germany he had studied anatomy and given art lessons to his fellow prisoners and, after the war, he taught figure drawing and landscape painting to Kendal Art Society.

Bunty's drawings attracted him immediately.

'She could draw extremely well,' he said, 'but her paintings were leathery and dull. She was mixing her colours with raw linseed oil and I persuaded her to boil them up with litharge [lead monoxide], to give them luminosity and make them more transparent.'

Robin Bagot introduced her to other painters. She met Claude Harrison from Grasmere, a highly traditional painter and a member of the Royal Society of Portrait Painters, and Bardy Crewdson, a portrait painter who, with her husband Peter, became Bunty's and Jimmy's life-long friends. At last, Bunty could indulge in 'the free flow of chatter

Bunty 1949. Portrait by Lenare.

which,' according to Robin Bagot, 'stimulates painting'.

He encouraged her to exhibit in the Kendal Art Society's Annual Exhibition in the Town Hall in 1951. She was overjoyed when the critic of the *Lancashire Evening Post* chose her portrait *The Girl in the Green Scarf*, a study of their German au-pair, Ursula, as one of the finest paintings in the exhibition – although in his write-up he called the scarf grey, not green.

It was an unerring choice and Robin Bagot's confidence in Bunty was more than justified, for that first painting exhibited publicly was destined to receive international recognition when chosen by the Royal Society of Portrait Painters for their travelling exhibition and, two years later, shown in the Paris Salon.

The local art critic was less sure of himself when he wrote about her second painting in the show which would, one day, earn comparable approval. He inaccurately entitled it *Treasure of Venus,* and thought it 'an unusual picture which is a reproduction of a sea shell and what I take to be a mermaid's coil of hair'.

In fact, Bunty's *Still Life for Venus*, the other half of her amazing public début, was an allegorical interpretation of her favourite painting, Botticelli's *The Birth of Venus*, a reproduction of which always hung in her home. Botticelli's naked maiden, discreetly shrouded by

PAINTING

Augustus John said of a portrait of himself by Matthew Smith 'Another haemorrage from Matthew, all the same he will be a portrait painter yet'.

A painting is finished when you're bored with it –
Augustus John.

It is an allowable generalization that an artist is one on whom life makes an impression unusually exciting & profound.

PAINTING is make-believe – not reality.
LOWRY. June 12th

Mother of Pearl
1962.
Oil on panel.

her long fair hair, rose from the sea in a scallop shell while a crimson cloak waited to envelop her. Bunty's picture showed a plait of golden hair and an elaborate conch shell arranged on a length of coral-coloured damask draped over a rock. The contrast in textures was masterly and imaginative, as was the conception. It had been achieved after days of painstaking work, sometimes using a brush with just two hairs.

This painting was the forerunner for the imaginative little still lifes that would be her acknowledged forté. They came from her 'world of ideas' which, according to Peter Crewdson, a sound art lover, 'is represented in pictures which drew upon her surprising capacity for doggedly and painstakingly seeking perfection in the minutiae of their composition. They were never radical or, in any sense, *avant garde*, but as remarkable in their make-up as in the meticulous manner of their composition.'

Crewdson, chairman of a local

engineering company and a High Sheriff of Cumbria, was one of the very few people who suspected that Bunty was at pains to avoid appearing intellectual.

'But her intelligence kept flashing through,' he said, 'in her robust and sometimes mordant wit.' And also in pictures like *Still Life for Venus* which she gave to her sister, Pamela.

Bunty found that painting her exquisite little still lifes was far more physically demanding than painting large portraits. With still life she permitted herself no concession and worked until she was completely satisfied with the result, while with portraits, her unfailing gift for catching a likeness compensated for any technical shortcomings.

Sometimes, her commissioned portraits were too conventional and rather stilted. Peter Crewdson felt that might be because, perhaps unconsciously, she was conforming to the strict social customs in which she had been brought up. He was her life-long admirer and saw her as ' ... a sensual and loving being who, I think, used the protection of conventional behaviour in which she had been brought up, to shield and protect her profound and inner self.

Shauna Fitzroy
Daughter of Lord and Lady Edward Fitzroy. Oil on canvas.

'Her movements were graceful and stately, in the belief that "women and cows should not run".

'In her case still waters ran very deep, and whether she had any radical thoughts or not they did not appear in her art or in her more public behaviour.'

Privately however, despite Bunty's conventional upbringing by a mother who did not allow her to paint nude figures, she displayed among her circle of close friends a full-blown version of a schoolboy's coarse sense of humour. Her only motive was to engender laughter.

Sir Giles Guthrie Bt
Chairman of B.O.A.C. 1955.

There was the memorable centrepiece she created for a dinner party – a bright green fountain-like effigy that dominated the table. Only on close scrutiny did her guests realise that it was a large cucumber carved into a phallic symbol, rising from a bed of lettuce shredded into fronds like fine hairs. Her elderly neighbour, Cecil Partridge, an antique dealer and a long-time widower, gave a birthday party. Bunty arrived with her present of a life-sized rag doll which had taken her days to create. The voluptuous female effigy was dressed in a beautiful set of removable garments and her striptease act was the success of the evening.

Cecil Partridge told Bunty that he much preferred her pictures to those of his niece who regularly exhibited portraits. and flower paintings in the Royal Academy. He asked Bunty to paint his portrait and sat for her in his drawing-room full of priceless antiques. It was her first request for a portrait and she thought him a great character. However, in her over-ambitious attempt to incorporate antique furniture into the background, she did less than justice in the painting to the lovable eccentric whose vulgar turn of phrase, at times, matched her own.

Cecil invited Sir Harold Parkinson, Vice-chairman of the British National Savings Committee, and Lady Parkinson to see Bunty's work. As a result, on 31st October, 1949, Sir Harold sent his Rolls-Royce to take her to his home, Hornby Castle, where she spent four days painting his portrait. It was her first major commission.

... am terrified, she wrote to her parents. *However, he's so kind and sweet and I am getting 30 gns. Cecil says he's*

Lady Guthrie
Painted nine years after her husband for their silver wedding.

sure if I do this well, Sir H.P. will put me on to <u>heaps</u> of people.

Cecil was right. A stream of commissions followed including one from other neighbours, the Earl and Countess Peel, to paint their portraits. Lord Peel, formerly Lord Lieutenant of Lancashire, was a great-grandson of Sir Robert Peel, the Home Secretary whose reorganisation of the London Police Force resulted in policemen being known as 'Bobbies' or 'Peelers'. More than a century later, however, their successors in the force failed to prevent a daring robbery or succeed in catching the culprits. As a

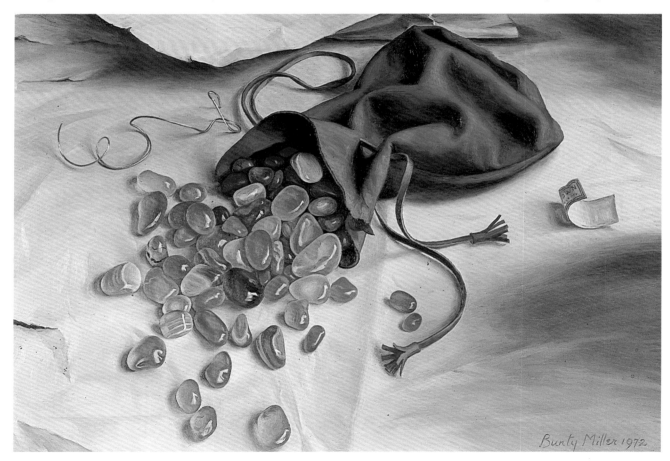

Bunty Miller 1968.

Snowdrops **picked at Surlingham. Exhibited at the Royal Academy 1968. Oil on panel.**

result, Bunty Miller's portrait of the Countess became the only visual reminder of a potential family heirloom.

For the portrait, Lady Peel chose to wear her favourite jewellery. It was a magnificent set of emeralds, five pieces valued at more than £40,000, which her husband had given her after the birth of their eldest son in 1947.

Bunty preferred her sitters to wear casual clothes but, in this case, their formal dress was amply compensated for by the opportunity it gave her to capture the play of light on the sparkling emerald and diamond necklace from which hung a brilliant square-cut stone, said to be one of the finest emeralds in the world.

Usually Lady Peel's jewels were stored in the safe deposit at Carringtons, the Royal jewellers in London's Regent Street. They were there during the weekend in 1965 when thieves raided the strong-room and emptied it of an estimated £500,000 worth of jewellery, including a tiara given by Napoleon to his second wife, two items valued at £20,000 belonging to Lady Docker and Lady Peel's under-insured emeralds which were never seen again.

Lie still, lie still, my breaking heart;
my silent heart, lie still and break;
Life, and the world, and mine own self,
are changed
for a dream's sake.
Christina Rossetti.

It was an upsetting day for Bunty when a buyer came to collect a commissioned painting.

'Mum would just disappear,' said Undine. 'She was very shy about showing anyone a picture they had commissioned and I was the one who, from an early age, had to hand them over to their new owners. Mum would hide upstairs or go out. Her work was very personal to her and she was extremely nervous as to how it would be received – much more so with portraits than with anything else.'

Bardy Crewdson confirmed this.

'She found commissioned portraits very unnerving,' she said, 'but did them to earn the money. But when, like Bunty, you've had no training, you really need years of experience in drawing and painting to compensate.'

While Bunty was nurturing her un-developed talent she perhaps feared criticism, except from the family.

'She was never satisfied with her own work,' Undine said. 'She was always asking our opinion. At the end of a day's work, when she was tired and the light was going and her brushes were drying, she'd say, "Darling, what do you think?" She constantly wanted Dad's or my opinion and she always took our advice.'

Bunty's modesty – or insecurity – about her work was evidenced by a brilliant self-portrait, the frontispiece to this book. It was painted when she was in her early thirties, but no one knew of its existence until after her death, when the family discovered it hidden in the attic.

During their first years at Hyning, the children went to the village school and Bunty was at last free to spend all day in her studio, converted from a bedroom.

'We weren't particularly well off,' said Undine, 'but there was always some inadequate person to help in the house. I remember we had an Italian waiter, a German au pair and, once, an ex-prostitute.'

Bunty painted feverishly, often from six o'clock in the morning until well into the evening.

'She had tremendous powers of observation and concentration,' Bardy Crewdson recalled. 'She painted commissioned portraits because she felt she had to, although she much preferred doing those beautiful little groups of small objects. It was still life in the most minute detail.'

It was certainly slow and painstaking work. So delicate was the brushwork and so slow the progress that, sometimes, Jimmy would be able to detect no change in a picture after Bunty had been working on it all day in the studio.

Robin Bagot understood her talent.

'She was far too much of a realist to come to terms with landscape,' he said.

Confirming this Peter Crewdson described seeing Bunty and Bardy out painting together: 'Bardy was focussed miles away, painting the landscape, while Bunty was concentrating on a single poppy.'

Robin Bagot said, 'She could copy everything she saw, down to the most minute detail. Her real love was for small beautiful things and, once she found the right medium and learnt to handle those fine brushes, she used her acute vision and incredible delicacy of handling most effectively.

'Those single threads of cotton in her pictures would have delighted the old Dutch Masters. Like them, her forté was deceptive realism so you felt you could touch the little objects she had painted. A sign of the Dutch influence was the way she sometimes painted handwriting into a picture.

'Personally, I never ceased to be amazed that the over-generous Bunty, with her bountiful handwriting should concentrate on such minute details. Also, that such a very lovely and amusing woman should have such a very earthy sense of humour.'

Mixing with experienced painters made Bunty even more aware of her limitations. Robin Bagot, mindful that she had never attended life classes nor studied anatomy, introduced her to a lavishly illustrated book, *The Art and Craft of Drawing* by Vernon Blake. It traced drawing from primitive times and showed details of figure drawing, shadow perspective, composition and even the various methods of holding a

Love is the light and sunshine of life.
We cannot fully enjoy ourselves, or anything else unless someone we love enjoys it with us.

♡ "I like not only to be loved but also to be told that I am loved..."
George Eliot.

paintbrush in ancient Egypt, India and China.

It was Jimmy, however, who gave her her most important textbook, *The Materials of the Artist and their Use in Painting,* translated from a 1921 German publication by Max Doerner, Professor of Fine Arts at the Munich Academy. It explained the techniques of the Old Masters and, for ever after, it became her bible.

For easy reference, she stuck permanent little markers into the pages where she underlined some of the techniques she planned to adopt. Many endorsed Robin Bagot's comment that, for her, 'Rubens was a God'.

She read that the luminosity in his paintings such as *The Straw Hat* came from mixing the best possible white with his colours; that the tint of the skin tones was achieved by using sienna, not vermilion, and the transparency of his brown was the result of mixing it with gold ochre. The textured effects, as in the ostrich feathers she had admired were, she read, achieved by painting the light tones opaquely, as solid bodies, and by using glazes for the shadows.

Rubens' method of mixing his colours was much as Robin Bagot had suggested. But in place of his laboriously prepared canvasses, for Bunty's still lifes Jimmy cut wooden panels to size and covered them with three or four layers of gesso, (a mixture of chalk and glue), and sandpapered them down to a very smooth surface.

As well as learning, from the book, about the colours and glazes used by the world's greatest painters, she adopted the advice to place a mirror to show the model and the picture at the same time so that, while she worked, she could check her drawing mistakes and the proportions of light and shadow. After this discovery she always worked with an elegant little floor-standing adjustable mirror at her shoulder.

A less practical, but more fundamental, passage in the book told her that *'an artist must be moved solely by inspiration ... Art is not a matter of either mind alone or handicraft alone, but a vision of both.'*

She heavily marked that passage in red ink.

It could certainly have applied to a romantic still life in oils called *Driftwood and Shells* which, again encouraged by Robin Bagot, she tentatively submitted to the Royal Scottish Academy in 1952. To her amazement it was accepted, and the following year *Still Life for Venus* hung there in mitigation of the local paper's rather confused comment when it had been shown in the Kendal Art Society's Exhibition.

The stream of commissions escalated. One was for a portrait of the Earl of Lonsdale for his eighty-fifth birthday. He lived in nearby Lowther Castle and was a great character who had been a

King's Messenger in the First World War. He had inherited the title from an elder brother Hugh, known as 'The Yellow Earl' because, since the thirteenth century, yellow had been the family colour as reflected in the servants' livery and in vehicles from horse-drawn carriages to Rolls-Royces. When Hugh became the first President of the Automobile Association they adopted his colour in their symbols. It was he who conceived the Lonsdale Belt award and he once fought a duel in Hyde Park over Lily Langtry.

Like him, his heir was very fond of the ladies.

'Oh! I wish you were my doxy,' he told Bunty at the first sitting, and in her picture she captured the twinkle in his eyes. They were strangely reminiscent of the glistening eyes of Cornelius van der Geest in Van Dyke's portrait which she

Eggs from Bixley commemorating the many times the Colman family left gifts of eggs on the artist's doorstep. Exhibited at the Royal Academy 1978. Oil on canvas.

had so admired.

Sittings took place after lunch, with Lord Lonsdale comfortably relaxed in his armchair, smoking a cigar. Invariably, he was soon fast asleep. One afternoon Bunty noticed that the lighted cigar had slipped from his fingers onto his trousers.

'It was starting to smoulder,' she said, 'and I had to take pretty smart action to stop it from burning his crotch. I was quite terrified in case someone walked in while I was trying to cope and got the wrong impression.'

Another commission came from Miki Sekers, the Hungarian refugee and music patron whose skills in textile manufacture had brought much-needed employment to West Cumberland. Bunty visited his home at Whitehaven:

... *a glorious Georgian house*, she wrote, *with superb and fabulous decorations, a Dégas pastel, an early Picasso, a Dufy oil, two John Pipers, three Oliver Messels – all originals needless to say, and a gorgeous Bohemian (un-county English) atmosphere.*

LOVE

Set me as a seal upon thine heart, as a seal upon thine arm; for love is strong as death; jealousy is cruel as the grave; the coals thereof are coals of fire, which hath a most vehement flame. Many waters cannot quench love neither can the floods drown it.

Solomon's Song
viii, 6 — 7.

The supreme happiness of life is the conviction that we are loved.

Victor Hugo.

Miki Sekers invited her to design a range of brocades for his new collection.

Oh, but I'm so LUCKY and it's very naughty of me to grouse, she wrote to her parents.

But the invitation had come just when she and Jimmy were preparing for their first holiday in Italy – a present from her parents. She already had to finish a commissioned oil study of white clematis before they left.

... and so, darlings, I'm going to have my hands full, she wrote in a mood of unusual despondency. *We simply CANNOT afford to risk losing ANY opportunity. It's all such a nightmare this money business – that it's imperative I don't miss a single chance. And really, it IS a chance in a life-time. Anyway, I will just have to go to the Mill and work all the night on the designs if need be.*

I dare say I just arrange my life messily – but the fact remains that it is a continuous struggle – often joyous, but always a necessary struggle. It's V tricky to arrange this dual existence successfully – and never to neglect anyone or anything – and go to bed each night with a clear conscience.

It was invariably after midnight when she went to bed while she was designing the delicate sprays of seaweed, lady's lace and dandelion clocks in various

The life that I have
Is all that I have
And the life that I have is yours –
The love that I have
Of the life that I have
Is yours and yours and yours.
A sleep I shall have
A rest I shall have
Yet death will be but a pause,
For the peace of my years
In the long green grass
Will be yours and yours and yours.
Leo Marks.

colour combinations for Miki Sekers' West Cumberland Silk Mills. Jimmy helped her to work out the mathematical proportions required for the Jacquard-woven material. Finally, he got up at six o'clock in the morning and drove for two hours to deliver the designs to the mill on time. It was a proud moment for Bunty when she sent her mother a length of silvery brocade woven with her own design for an evening gown.

The Italian trip was memorable. She and Jimmy stayed with family friends in Florence and, in the Uffizi, Bunty was at last confronted by Botticelli's *The Birth of Venus* which had been her early inspiration. It's vivid beauty outshone anything she had imagined from the reproductions. In Florence, she was dazed by Michelangelo's gigantic *David* and by his ceiling in the Vatican's Sistine Chapel. There were other trips to Italy, including one to Venice, where their hotel overlooked St Marco and where she was almost overwhelmed by the wonders of the Tintorettos, the Canalettos, the Bellinis and the other great Italian masters, as well as by the splendour of the Italian skies over the lagoon and the sheer flamboyance of the Venetian sunset. But from that first visit to Italy she returned with a new perspective and fresh sense of determination.

It was short-lived. Eight-year-old Colin went to prep school near Carlisle and, suddenly, the happy life-style at Hyning was jeopardised. Bunty, a devoted mother, found the sixty mile separation from her son intolerable and his exeats left her drained of all creative energy.

I always feel numb with sadness when we leave him, she wrote to her parents. *Somehow, it's a most terrific strain not saying 'Hello my darling' and clasping him to me when we meet. Instead he advanced towards the car quite dignifiedly (no wild enthusiastic rush) but quietly pink in the face with pleasure. And we say 'Hello' to each other as if we'd met a few hours before.*

And what seems hours later I kiss him guardedly. He hates us leaving him but there's not much said. And by the time we drop him he can't speak for the lump in his throat, I know.

The last few hours he casually asks us the time a little too often with unconvincing nonchalance. He just gets out of the car, raises his cap to us and, without a word or a backward glance, he walks into school.

Well, that simply does something to my heart. I can't feel it's right – 'tho I agree it's inevitable – for a child of that age to have to control his feelings and emotions to that extent. When I think of the years that this has got to go on for, I feel quite overwhelmed.

Such emotional upsets contributed to the lack of energy, resulting from her persistent thyroid trouble. She had two thyroid operations within a short time which improved matters, but still she was often so tired at the end of the day that Jimmy cleaned her brushes and palette when he came home.

For financial reasons, there was no

question of sending Undine to boarding school. A convenient compromise was offered by Sandford School at Witherslack, a girls' boarding school five miles from Hyning, prepared to take Undine as their only day girl providing she lived in the village. So the Millers rented an unprepossessing isolated greystone house, The Lawns at Witherslack, a hundred and fifty yards from the school.

While awaiting vacant possession they lived for a few months in a three-roomed cottage near Kendal. It was too

Barrister's Wig **worn by the artist's son-in-law. Hung 'on the line' at the Royal Academy 1966. Oil on panel.**

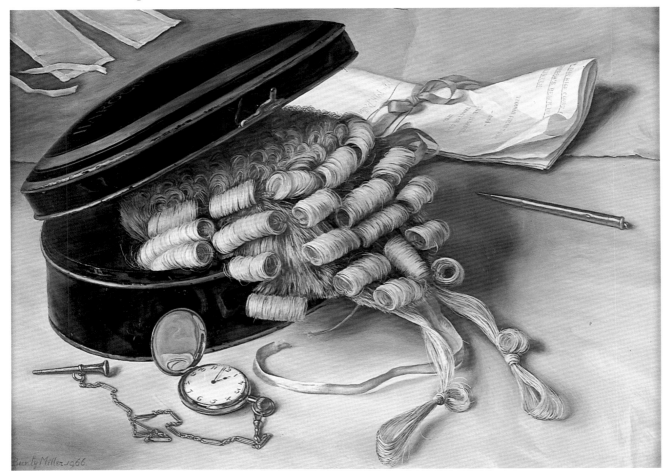

Fear is the most disintegrating enemy of human personality – & worry is the most subtle and distructive of all human diseases.

small to have a living-in help, so Bunty resigned herself to doing all the housework, cooking and washing and the ironing and mending again. It took her all day, and at first she was quite happy.

'It's very sweet and cosy here and brings out the Mrs Tiggywinkle in me,' she told her parents. But the novelty was short-lived.

The date for taking over The Lawns was repeatedly delayed and Bunty, with no energy to paint, again grew uncharacteristically despondent.

I've seriously thought of giving up painting completely, she wrote to her parents, *and devote myself entirely to the family and so avoid the dual existence and the constant emotional strain. At the moment I can't contemplate painting for a while at least. There's so much to be done – and it's really hopeless trying to be too many things at once and doing none of them really well.*

She was a perfectionist, in her work and her relationships with her family and friends, which often resulted in an energy-sapping conflict. 'If you have talent and energy you are a king. But if you have talent and no energy you are a pauper,' was a quotation she passed on to Bardy. Both agreed that the one quality a woman painter needed was the capacity to be selfish, in order to concentrate totally on her work, despite the intrusion of family problems and the responsibility of creating a home. It was a quality that both completely lacked.

Bunty's parents, who had decided to live in Jersey, invited the family to spend their summer holiday with them, with their fares paid. Bunty declined, 'after hours of thought and discussion,' she said.

I've been dreading putting it down on paper, she wrote to them, *but you see all the money which would be for a holiday could buy us one or two of the things we badly need for The Lawns. If only you knew how desperately disappointing it is for us all, my darlings.*

Her twenty-page letter enumerated everything they needed for their first completely unfurnished rented home. With new school uniforms for the children, riding clothes for Undine and a new suit for Jimmy the move would take all their savings, she said.

Moreover, once again, Bunty had no time to paint and supplement their

42

income. To add to her problems, Colin was sent home from school to convalesce after a burst appendix and a spell in hospital where he nearly died, and Bunty hardly left his bedside. When he came home she took the opportunity to paint his portrait and produced a rather stiff likeness of a wan little boy in school uniform. He hated being away at school.

The dull portrait was in marked contrast to a vibrant study of Undine painted a few years later when life was running more smoothly again. Bunty saw her daughter coming from the bathroom, swathed in a large towel, her hair caught up in a pony-tail.

'I must paint you just like that,' she exclaimed, and in an hour and a quarter she had completed the portrait in full colour with no under-painting or drawing. She simply applied wet on wet and allowed the light ground to come through to give brightness and luminosity to the skin tone.

'Don't add another brushstroke,' Robin

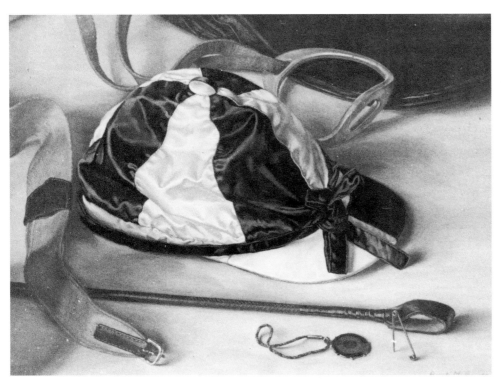

Jockey Cap - which resulted in a spate of requests for similar pictures from racehorse owners after it was exhibited at the Royal Academy in 1966. Oil on panel.

Bagot said, in unstinting approval of her first brilliant attempt at painting *alla prima,* a process she had underlined in her old text book.

It aims from the very start, she had read, *at the final effect of the finished picture and attempts to arrive at that effect in the shortest and most direct way ... Among the older schools it was the crowning achievement, the ultimate in craftsmanship ... the fruit of long preparation and could be undertaken only with complete knowledge of the rules of the craft, as a brilliant summary of all the technical processes of picture building.*

Bunty's spontaneous venture into 'the ultimate in craftsmanship' could hardly

Pearls and Paper
Exhibited at the Royal Academy 1987.
A last Academy exhibit.
Oil on board.

have been 'a brilliant summary of all the technical processes' so much as proof of her instinctive ability. It indicated that the scope of her painting could have been widely extended had she not confined herself to producing the charming little still lifes for which, she knew, there was an insatiable demand, and the commissioned portraits which were necessary intrusions.

In 1955, through an introduction from Pamela's husband, Peter Sykes, she was invited to paint a portrait of Sir Giles Guthrie, Bt., Chairman of B.O.A.C. The commission, for which she was paid £126, led to a close and lifelong friendship with Lady Guthrie.

They met for the first time when Bunty went to their home at Gatwick to discuss the portrait.

'This gorgeous creature walked in,' Rhona Guthrie recalled, 'and I thought, "how on earth can such an exquisite person really produce serious work?"

'I decided to get down to brass tacks straight away and ask how much she charged for a portrait?

'"That depends," she said. "It's so much for a full-length portrait, so much for head and shoulders and somewhere in between if you only want it down to the crotch."

'She stayed with us for a fortnight to paint the portrait and I grew completely captivated by her. She was an original. Spontaneously witty with a raunchy, robust sense of humour, warm, loving

Beauty Miller 1966

and compassionate and extremely sensitive. She was the best listener I've ever come across, and if ever I wanted to let off steam she'd just listen and be wonderfully sympathetic.

'Of course, as her pictures show, she was a perfectionist with limitless patience. She took the scales from my

Violets
Exhibited at the Royal Academy 1966. Oil on panel.

> "A friend is one to whom one can pour out all the contents of ones heart, chaff & grain together - knowing that the gentlest of hands will take & sift it - keep what is worth keeping and with a breath of kindness blow the rest away." Arabian Proverb.

eyes again and again. I remember we were walking through the fields and she picked a dandelion. "What perfection!" she said and took a magnifying glass out of her pocket and showed me every minute detail. She taught me to see life in a completely different light.

'Yet, at the same time, she was tremendous fun to be with. She had a wonderful sense of the absurd. Once we dressed up as men with wigs and painted moustaches on each other and went out on the town.

'Another time we stuffed lemons down our bras like a couple of school kids. The thing I remember most is the laughter that always seemed to surround her, and also her talent for making me and other people feel wonderful.'

The Guthries, like so many of Bunty's sitters, became her firm friends. Nine years after Bunty had painted Giles, she did a companion portrait of Rhona for their silver wedding. The two couples went on many holidays together, often in the Guthrie's ninety-foot motor cruiser, *Alitia*. She slept six plus a crew of four, but Rhona insisted that she and Bunty did all the cooking and for Bunty, a bad sailor, it was often quite an ordeal.

They cruised up the Albanian coast to Dubrovnik, sailed round the Norwegian Fjords and, for three summers, explored the Greek islands, where Bunty was sometimes left on her own for a few precious hours to paint. But for Bunty it was never long enough.

There was never enough time to paint and, at home, she came to rely more and more on the daughter who was far more domesticated than she was.

'I had to be,' Undine said. 'From a very early age I was cleaning and sweeping and cooking and clearing up after her dinner parties – doing many of the things that other mothers would probably have done, like bringing up my brother for much of the time, even if he was two years younger than I.

'I packed his trunks for school and did his washing and wrote to him on Sundays and sent him sweets because Mum was always trying to find time to paint.

'But I was not lacking in love or affection in any way. She was a marvellous mother and very attentive, and I only had to go and knock at the studio door and she'd be there, just waiting to listen.

'She was a wonderful listener and whenever anything happened in the family, whether it was sad or wonderful, she was the first person to ring. If it was something ghastly she'd cry with one and if it was wonderful she'd be crying just the same, but with tears of joy. So, all my life, I had somebody to ring and share things with.'

Bunty's family and friends felt the same, and an ever-escalating problem for her was the conflicting demands of painting and social and family affairs. Whenever anyone was ill she'd drop everything to go and help.

'She saw me through several spells in hospital,' Bardy Crewdson said. 'She was the closest friend I ever had. I was desperately distressed when they left Cumbria.'

They left in 1958 when Jimmy was posted to Cambridge. Colin was, by then, at the Nautical College, Pangbourne, his father's old school. Undine went to the Cambridge Technical College to study art and home was a house in Thornton Road, Girton, with a wooden shed in the garden for a makeshift studio. There Bunty painted a picture that set a pattern for a lifetime of public acclaim.

Red Taffeta Rose showed a freshness of texture and a romantic originality, allied to perfection of detail that would become the hallmarks of her success. In 1959, it hung in the Royal Academy's Summer Exhibition and was sold early in the morning of the first private view day.

LOVE

Falling in love is sudden, strong, compulsive, largely irrational. Often it's frightening, as is any explosive emotion. A girl may feel — as a woman — tongue-tied, limp, almost helpless near the man she loves. A telephone call, a word of encouragement, a smile or a touch brings on a sense of elation. In fact a thriving love affair acts for most people as a powerful, primitive tonic; it actually stimulates physical and emotional health. So it is not surprising that reason frequently flies out of the mind when love appears.....

Bowl of Roses
A present from the artist to
her sister Pamela.
Oil on panel.

That auspicious début resulted in a deluge of enquiries, from members of the public wanting to buy similar paintings, from gallery owners keen to show her work and, most satisfying of all, a request from the Medici Society to be allowed to reproduce the painting as a greetings card. They offered her £20 and fifty copies of the card for the new owner of the painting.

She wrote immediately to the merchant banker who had bought it.

I was terribly excited at the thought of my picture being reproduced in colour – and also – I must confess, thankful at the thought of the extra £20 <u>until</u> I realised that, of course, the picture is <u>yours</u> now – and therefore the £20 too.

I am writing to ask if you will be <u>very</u> kind and allow this work of mine to be reproduced? I feel certain you will understand how much it will mean to me, and how it will help to further my career.

I do so HOPE that you will not have any objection to this suggestion. Please could you be good enough to let me know about this as soon as you conveniently can – for I can hardly wait to hear.

I wonder if you will understand when I tell you that I'm delighted (after a sort of anonymous wondering over the weekend) to know the identity of the new owner. It may well sound ridiculous to think of or imagine the future home of an inanimate object *– but one's work is almost one's* child ...

Permission to have the painting reproduced came by return. Bunty was delighted, particularly because, in her inexperience, she had not realised that, although she had sold the picture, she

Diana
The artist's daughter-in-law at the time of her engagement.
Oil on canvas.

still retained the copyright and therefore was entitled to the £20.

Her paintings epitomised romantic daintiness, underlaid by an earthy realism that protected them from any tendancy to sugary sweetness. Perhaps her own earthy realism attracted her to a grotesque portrait by Ruskin Spear in the same exhibition. It was the complete antithesis to her work yet she felt compelled to write and congratulate the artist. She wrote with a newfound confidence and artistic maturity:

I was walking round the galleries of the R.A. when suddenly your woman with the ice cream hit me almost as forcibly as if I had been in collision with some tangible object. I shall never be able to forget it and have thought of it constantly ever since, for it made such an enormous impression on me.

As I stood rivetted in front of the DREADFUL ridiculous woman – the pitiable and repellent epitome of material greed – I could almost hear her sucking and smell her sickeningly sweet scent, and the strawberry ice, everything in me rebelling in disgust at her slippery scarlet mouth – the unpowdered and terrible face she was so busily filling, the fat, evil, jewelled hand. Oh! I can't find words to describe how impressively and wittily you have conveyed your disgust and how utterly BRILLIANT I think your work is – as indeed thousands will. It is yet another triumph. I imagine you did it in a matter of hours while the horror of this vision was still fresh in your mind?

Quite apart from the strength and purpose of the PAINT at which I marvel, the squareness of the work so cleverly emphasises the enormity of the subject. The whole thing is FULL of wit; a terrifying message to spoilt, bored and greedy women, and such an invigorating comment on some of them in 1959!

To me, your work has all the power and impact of Goya – without any of the blood and I look forward more than I can say to seeing it again tomorrow – and throughout the exhibition.

Few painters can have received a more sensitive and well expressed fan letter.

Coincidently, she saw blood in plenty when, true to her conviction that she should never refuse a challenge to extend her work, she accepted an invitation from a Cambridge ortho-paedic surgeon, Mr John Fairbank, to do anatomical drawings in the theatre while he operated. The results were workmanlike records of his operations, despite the fact that she had never had a lesson in anatomy in her life.

By the end of the year, however, Jimmy had been promoted, and they moved to East Anglia and an attractive cottage in the heart of Broadland. Broad Cottage, Surlingham was at the edge of the village, in a bend of the River Yare, and had a dyke leading through the marshes to a small stretch of tidal water that, in summer, was full of reed beds where night warblers sang. The broad was barely navigable, but they bought a little boat with an outboard motor for pottering about in the summer. Part of the house had been an old marshman's cottage and the tiled dairy in the other part was converted into Bunty's first custom-built studio.

She christened it by painting her seventeen-year-old nephew Adrian's portrait and three still lifes for the 1960 Summer Exhibition of the Royal Academy. The paintings again sold within the first hours of being shown.

At last Bunty had all the time in the world to paint, for both the children had left home. Undine had taken a flat in London to be near the junior barrister she had met when he was a law student at Cambridge. He was Mark Potter whose father, Professor Harold Potter, had been founder and Dean of the Faculty of Law at King's College, London University. They had become engaged in 1960 when Undine was nineteen and planned to marry when she was twenty-one. Colin was also in London working, very unhappily, in a small tea firm.

Jimmy and Bunty, new arrivals in Norfolk, had not had time to make friends or become involved in the local social life. Bunty, for the first and possibly the only stage in her life, could work completely undisturbed in her studio.

Her two paintings in the 1961 Royal Academy's Summer Exhibition brought a request from the Royal Society of Portrait Painters on behalf of a client, for any paintings she had of young women. She sent the portrait of Ursula which had made its début as *The Girl in the Green Scarf* in the Kendal Art Society's Exhibition three years previously.

The client bought it, but allowed it to tour England in the Society's travelling exhibition before he took possession. Meanwhile, a portrait of Bunty's niece, Angela, shown in their next London

Give all to Love;
Obey thy heart;
Friends, kindred, days,
Estate, good fame,
Plans, credit, & the muse —
Nothing refuse.

Exhibition, led to a romantic commission.

It came from Blair Stewart-Wilson, Equerry to the Duke of Gloucester, after he had taken his twenty-year-old fiancée, Mary Fox, to see his portrait in the same exhibition. It was January 1962, ten days before their wedding at St Michael's Church, Chester Square, London.

'It was a fine portrait by Cowan Dobson,' Mary recalled, 'but going round the exhibition I suddenly noticed a study of a young girl in a blue headscarf. I was fascinated by it. I said to Blair; "That painting is so different. If I were going to have my portrait painted that's the artist I'd choose."'

Blair Stewart-Wilson telephoned Bunty and asked if she would paint Mary's portrait. Bunty said she was sorry but she was too busy and, anyhow, she was tired of painting portraits. Blair persisted.

'You should just see her,' he said. 'She's got dark hair, blue eyes and rosy cheeks and we're getting married in ten days time and I want the picture for her wedding present.'

Bunty found the romantic appeal irresistible. Sittings began two days later at the home of one of the bride's friends. By that time, however, Mary was having

Angela Sykes (Mrs Douglas-Mann) – the artist's niece. Exhibited at the Royal Society of Portrait Painters 1962.

last minute misgivings about marrying an 'old man' of thirty-two.

Some thirty years later Mary Stewart-Wilson's husband was Deputy Master of the Royal Household, they had three daughters and Mary was the author of two successful books, *Queen Mary's Doll's House* and *The Royal Mews*.

'Bunty was wonderful,' Mary recalled. 'She managed to calm me down by pointing out the merits I'd never considered about marrying an older man. She was utterly reassuring.

'She was also very romantic and obviously tremendously in love with her husband. I felt that, for her, life was still seen in terms of a prince galloping in on a white charger. She held deeply romantic ideas about marriage and the way it enshrined one in love and mystery once the ring was on the bride's finger. If you loved someone and married, then you lived happily ever after.

'We talked non-stop for the whole week of the sittings, about so many things. I'd studied art in Florence and I found it fascinating to watch her work. She said she was always being complimented on the way she handled hair in her portraits. Anthony Devas had shown her how to paint hair, she said, when she sat to him for her own portrait.

'She gave me a practical tip; "From now on always use the same scent," she said "so wherever in the world Blair goes he'll think of you whenever he smells that scent." It was too late to invite her to the wedding but I said we'd love her to be there. She sent us a dear little pair of china rabbits for a present

Mary Stewart-Wilson - wife of the Deputy Master of the Royal Household - painted a week before their wedding in 1962.

> " ... All this, and the feeling that
> it would never end, that such
> days had come for ever ...
> All sights twice-brilliant and
> smells twice-sharp, all game-days
> twice as long ..." Laurie Lee.
> "Cider with Rosie".

and I heard she'd slipped into the back of the church for the wedding.

'We always remained loving friends and whenever we met I felt immensely refreshed. She was like a great cool well of kindness to drink from.'

The portrait must have been a striking likeness. Undine had never met Mary Stewart-Wilson although she remembered her mother working on the painting. A few years later she had built a sandcastle for her children near the sea at Trebetherick and was waiting for the tide to come in and fill the moat. It was a splendid castle, its turrets decorated with shells and seaweed and many passers-by stopped to admire it.

Suddenly she heard a man say, 'I'm afraid the tide's turned without filling the moat'.

She looked up at a complete stranger and, with a shock, recognised his companion although she had never met her before.

'Didn't my mother, Bunty Miller, once paint your portrait?' she asked Mary Stewart-Wilson.

'It was uncanny and, somehow, quite a spooky moment,' Undine recalled.

The year that Bunty painted the portrait, the Medici Society bought the reproduction rights of her two paintings in the Royal Academy's Summer Exhibition, *Spring Headdress* and *Red Silk Shoes*. The latter elicited an enormous fan mail; dealers again wanted to represent her, galleries offered to show her work and two fine art publishers asked to reproduce it on an enlarged scale. People wrote from all over the world keen to buy a similar picture and the Northampton College of Technology wanted one for their collection of paintings of shoes and shoe-makers.

Bunty was not interested. Only in very special circumstances would she copy a picture she had painted and, instinctively, she shied away from committing her small, extremely personal paintings to galleries or having them blown up in size. In any case, she was selling everything she painted.

She did, however, accept an invitation from a publisher to design jackets for a Book Club edition of *Cider with Rosie*, the Catholic Book Club editions of *Approaches to Christian Unity* and *The*

One True Kirk and the Garden Book Club's *Tomato Growing by Prescription.* They were new challenges and a welcome contrast to her laboriously fine work.

A period of prolific painting was interrupted by Undine's wedding in August, 1962. Bunty was determined that everything should be perfect down to the last detail, which meant months of preparation. The reception was held in a marquee on the lawn of the home

Paper Boats
Exhibited at the Royal Academy 1973. Oil on board.

Bunty Miller, 1973

Daisy Chain
Exhibited at the Royal
Academy 1975.
Oil on panel.

Pamela and Peter had bought, near Norwich, in order to be near Bunty on Peter's retirement.

It was autumn before Bunty could start work again, on a portrait of Shauna Fitzroy, the little daughter of Lord Edward Fitzroy, the brother of the Duke of Grafton. She also worked on the book jackets and on three paintings for the Royal Academy – the maximum number she was allowed to submit to the selection committee. They were an imaginative study of a camellia, a bouquet of flowers and a plume of coral feathers, echoing Ruben's swirling feathers worn by the lady in *The Straw Hat*. All three were accepted. They were her entrée to the world she loved, and

Bunty Miller 1977.

The Old Flag
A tribute to the Royal
Jubilee. Exhibited at the
Royal Academy 1977.
Oil on panel.

the Academy was the only shop window she ever needed.

On Varnishing Day she was in her element.

'It was her day,' Undine said, 'a very special day when she had no family to think about. She'd come down on the train to London with a basket containing all her painting things, and she had a lovely flirty time with all those interesting artists who were always wanting to paint her portrait.

'The day started with a service at St James's Church in Piccadilly and then they'd walk along to the Academy to see where their pictures had been hung. Everyone chatted and congratulated each other. It was her world – nothing to do with the family – and she'd come home on a sort of high.

'Private View Day and Opening Day were also very exciting. We'd all rush to the small South Room to see her pictures, and when she saw the red stickers she was immensely relieved. I don't remember a year when they weren't all sold within the first few hours.

SUMMER

"The air of the place ...
thrilled all the while
with the bliss of birds,
the hum of little lives unseen
and the flicker
. of white butterflies ... "

Henry James.
" The Awkward Age ".

'She could have charged much more, but she wasn't greedy. Money was an anathema to her. She never thought about the price until the day before she had to send the pictures in. Mum, Dad, Mark and I would sit round the kitchen table with the pictures in front of us and discuss the price. We'd argue for hours. Mum would drop the price and we'd drift it up again. They were grossly under-priced because she'd taken weeks, and sometimes a month, to paint one small picture and, of course, she and Dad needed the money.'

When Bunty first exhibited in the Royal Academy, Private View Day was a highlight of the London Season and everyone dressed accordingly. The ladies wore gloves and hats and Bunty always created a hat to her own fey taste – usually a large straw with a real rose on it. She liked to look slightly original, not dressed as a fashion plate, invariably in one of the four colours she knew suited her best; aquamarine, creamy buttermilk, dark green and navy. She looked the epitome of romantic femininity and knew it.

The pattern was set for three, and occasionally two, Bunty Miller paintings in the Royal Academy each year for the next twenty-three years, with would-be purchasers vying to be the first to buy them.

'They weren't the sort of pictures to make the National Gallery but, some-how, you just couldn't bear to leave them behind,' said a proud purchaser.

In 1965, two pictures were of completely different types of hats; one was a jockey's cap in crimson and white quarters with a stirrup, girth, whip and, characteristically for the pin-loving Bunty, a tie pin; the other was a green flat-brimmed straw decorated with a satin ribbon and a pink rose.

Bunty could have painted jockey caps

in the colours of wealthy horse owners from all over the world for the rest of her life had she accepted all the requests that poured in. She turned them down, true to her maxim never to 're-live' a picture. With the straw hat, however, it was a different story.

When the distinguished writer Paul Gallico and his wife saw the picture in the Academy, sadly for them, it bore the inevitable red 'sold' dot. It portrayed just the sort of hat they envisaged being worn by Paul's famous fictitious character, Mrs Ada Harris, the indomitable cockney char who 'did' for a fashionable London clientele.

Three books about her had been best sellers on both sides of the Atlantic and a fourth was on the way. The first one, *Flowers for Mrs Harris,* had been inspired by a visit the author and his then bride-to-be, the Baroness Virginia von Falz-Fein, had made to Paris where Virginia had been fitted for a dress at the House of Christian Dior.

It had been Paul's introduction to the world of high fashion. Driving home to England he had ruminated on what would happen if Virginia's cleaning lady, Katie Fairman, a great character who had worked for her for twenty-four years, decided that she would like to have a Dior gown.

'I said that, somehow, she'd manage to get one,' Virginia recalled. 'If she wanted a thing badly enough she'd work until she got it.

'You see, I saw Katie Fairman as a sort of Mrs Everywoman for whom, like Cinderella, the most far-fetched dreams would sometimes come true.'

Paul Gallico liked the idea and so Katie Fairman became the model for his fictitious Mrs Harris. In his first book she flew to Paris, clutching all her savings in a battered imitation leather handbag and fulfilled a compelling ambition to buy a Dior dress.

HOPE

Within ourselves we have a hope which always walks in front of our present narrow experience — It will never accept any of our disabilities as a permanent fact; it sets no limit to it's own scope; and it's wild dreams become true every day.

Rabindrath Tagore.

Daffodils from Bixley
A wedding present for a
friend's daughter, Brina
Colman of Bixley Manor
Norwich, on her marriage
to Christopher Penn.
Oil on panel.

*It had not been a dream she had
bought,* Paul Gallico wrote, *so much as
an adventure and an experience that
would last her to the end of her days.*

In later books Mrs Harris travelled to
New York, to Moscow and finally
became an M.P., inspired by her initial
success as evidenced by a dress she
would never wear. Her hat, however,
remained the most significant part of
her wardrobe.

Only in the hat she wore, Gallico
wrote, *did her ebullient nature manifest
itself. It was of green straw and to the
front of it was attached the flexible stem
of a huge and preposterous rose which
leaned this way and that, seemingly
following the hand of the pilot upon the
wheel as the plane banked and circled ...
Anyone English would have said 'The
woman under that hat could only be a
London char'.*

Virginia Gallico wrote to Bunty

saying that she 'was enchanted' with the painting in the Royal Academy and asking if she would paint a similar one for a surprise birthday present for her husband in two months' time?

My husband is a writer, she explained, *and your painting represents all the* charm of Mrs Harris's hat in his books.

Bunty replied that she was unfortunately too busy with other commissions and family problems to paint a picture in time for the birthday.

Virginia Gallico persisted and conceded that perhaps it could be given as a

Mrs Harris's Hat
As worn by Paul Gallico's famous charlady and immortalised in three best-selling books.

Christmas present. Bunty capitulated. Telephone calls and letters followed with suggestions as to how the painting could be 'full of Mrs Harris's feelings'.

Bunty delivered the picture to the Gallicos in London in person. She had illustrated 'Mrs Harris's feelings' by including a pansy for remembrance and a front door key labelled with her address, '5, Willis Gardens, Battersea, London,' alongside the hat. She had so enjoyed the commission that she took along a small Christmas present for the Gallicos of a gondolier's tiny gilt hat, the same shape as Mrs Harris's, decorated with a miniature rose.

Paul and Virginia Gallico were thrilled with the picture and, Virginia wrote, touched by the gift. Soon afterwards, Paul invited Bunty to design the jacket for his new book, *The Man Who Was Magic*. She chose to illustrate the 'fable of faith and innocence' with another rose, quite unlike Mrs Harris's artificial one. It was a velvety white bloom with a dew drop on a petal. It grew from a thick oak staff and represented one of the Magic Man's tricks; to make roses sprout from his staff to prove the impossible was possible.

Bunty had not been just making excuses when she said, initially, that she was too busy with family problems to paint the picture. It was the year her father died and her mother moved to Norwich to be near her two daughters. Fay had married Sir Joscelyn Simon in 1948 who, eleven years later, became Solicitor General. They lived in London and Yorkshire.

To add to Bunty's worries, Colin had given up his job with the tea firm, partly because he hated living in London, and had decided to work his way round the world for at least a year. He had had no training in anything and Bunty was concerned about his future.

When he unpacked his suitcase at the start of his travels he found a letter folded in his pyjamas labelled *On your first night at sea from your adoring Mum*. In it Bunty had schooled herself to say how happy she was for him.

Your letters will be a joy, she wrote. *Tell us your THOUGHTS as well as your doings. If ever you're a bit miz don't hide it from us for we can write and comfort you. It'll just keep us going to know we can SHARE the odd tiresome times as*

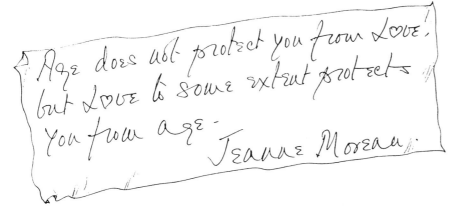

Age does not protect you from Love, but Love to some extent protects you from age. — Jeanne Moreau

well as the GOOD times ... I shall be with you in thought always.

She exhorted him to say his prayers, never get arrogant or big-headed or thoughtless for others, and share with her the motto she tried hard to live by; 'Do As You Would Be Done By' from *The Water Babies* by Charles Kingsley. She was as upset as when he had first gone away to school.

Bunty's tremendous concern for people extended far beyond her immediate family. Her talent for being a good listener, compounded from her intense curiosity, a great interest in people, a shrewd insight and a deep-seated need for admiration and to receive love as well as give it, led her to become more and more involved in other people's lives often as their greatest confidante.

'I told her far more than I told my mother,' Pamela's son, Adrian said. 'As I grew up she was a great ally and quite unshockable. She was wonderfully warm and loving and a fairly level-headed sentimentalist – too sensible to be a romantic.

'She always laughed and encouraged me and she could keep a secret very well. She had a talent for being able to flatter you by the quality of her listening. But, looking back, I think her involvement with others grew until it

> It is not the perfect, but the imperfect who have need of love.
> — Oscar Wilde

> Love seeketh not itself to please –
> Nor for itself hath any care,
> But for another gives its ease –
> And builds a heaven in hell's despair.
> — BLAKE

A broken fan belonging to Rhona Guthrie's mother-in-law painted fifteen years after it had been thrown out.
Oil on panel.

took up an immense amount of time and sapped her energy and her emotional resources.'

Distance was no deterrent. Often she was writing long chatty letters at five o'clock in the morning, and the telephone bills were enormous as she spent hours listening to the problems of her friends.

'She was the sort of person you rang up if a grandchild said something amusing or if you were in real trouble,' her neighbour and close friend, Lady Mary Colman, recalled. 'She was the confidante of all my five children and a wonderful help to them. She'd absorb your worries like a sponge. Whenever I went away there was always a "Welcome Home" card from her waiting when I got back. She was also a great present-giver.'

The time and thought that went into present-giving was illustrated by more than a dozen little ornaments and trinkets scattered around the Colman's home. With presents, as with everything that caught her interest, Bunty was a perfectionist. Some were the result of hours spent searching antique shops. Others were home-made, like a heart-shaped lace-edged pincushion with 'Happy Birthday Mary' and the date in pearl-headed pins and sequins; a shell-full of little stones she had collected and polished and a small glass dome containing a miniature silk flower arrangement embroidered with seed pearls and sequins.

Treasures from her shopping expeditions included an old tobacco tin embossed with 'M', a pair of antique posy vases, an enamel snuff box, a heart in beaten silver, a tiny silver envelope large enough to hold a postage stamp, a mother-of-pearl purse in which she had secreted an inscribed list of evocative words starting with 'M' and a pair of old glass bottles shaped like small crowns

Flowers from Stanley Mill collected in a friend's garden at Chippenham, Wiltshire.
Exhibited at the Royal Academy 1979.
Oil on panel.

FRIENDSHIP

Friendship improves Happiness
and abates Misery, by the doubling
of our Joy and dividing of our Grief.

Joseph Addison.
1672 – 1719.

♡———♡

Those who like the same things find
it the hardest thing in the world not
to like each other.

Logan Pearsall Smith.

♡

In friendship, nobody has a doubt.

F. Schiller.

♡———♡

Our friends show us what we can do; our
enemies teach us what we must do.

Goethe.

which she had filled with pale green water.

Her friends often received beautiful little water-colours on their birthdays or at Christmas, or for their children's christenings. Weddings warranted oil paintings. Adrian sent her the first page of a large Visitor's Book from his new home, asking her to paint 'a visual commentary' on his life. She filled the page with tiny studies representing his country interests. They included a salmon fly, a grouse feather, sprigs of heather and bracken and a pheasant's feather – all exquisitely painted.

'It was not water-colour paper,' he said, 'and those little watercolours must have taken her weeks to do because the paper wouldn't absorb the paint and she had to wait for each colour to dry before she could apply the next. But she was a perfectionist. That's a terrible disease ... '

Adrian perceived that as Bunty grew older she read more. Gradually her visual skill extended to language and she used words like a picture.

'She came to love words,' he said, 'although earlier in life she was a very unlettered woman.'

She collected passages from writings she loved and stuck them into her Common Place Book which she kept under their bed. She drew and ornamented any sayings that particularly delighted her so that they looked as if they were on scraps of paper decorated with hearts and flowers.

When Rhona Guthrie's mother was ill, Bunty compiled an album of hand-drawn sayings for her and left the last few pages blank to encourage her to add her own favourites. She also painted a few pages with little water-colours for good measure. It was a typical Bunty time-consuming present.

It may have been coincidence, but during Colin's world tour, when he was not around to tell her she ought to be painting more, as he often did, she had only two pictures each year in the Royal Academy.

In 1966, both were hung 'on the line', an accolade which entitled Bunty to put glass over them. They were *Violets* and *Barrister's Wig*, a study of Mark Potter's wig which had once belonged to his father. Any hair fascinated Bunty, and alongside the wig she placed an un-named brief because lawyers were not allowed to advertise. She longed to give Mark and Undine the painting but needed the money.

On Private View Day it carried the predictable red dot which Bunty saw with mixed feelings – until she learned that it was the Potters who had bought the picture.

'We felt we couldn't bear to live without it,' Undine said. 'It showed Mark's gold pen with his bite mark on it and his watch at one o'clock because that was lunchtime.'

With delight Bunty painted Mark Potter's name on the brief for its new owners.

Eighteen months later a very different Colin returned from his travels. While working as a rancher in Canada, a copper-miner in Australia, picking avocados on an Israeli kibbutz and touring India and Afghanistan, he had formulated his ideas and had decided to become a sculptor. The knowledge that his mother, with no training, had succeeded in art encouraged him.

'I had always wanted to do something with my hands,' he said, 'and the fact that Mum painted so beautifully meant that I would have to do something completely different unless I could reach that standard.'

So Ayrton Pullan's artistic ability manifested itself in a fifth generation.

Colin's first sculpture was of Bunty's head, done while she was working in her studio.

'She was always tremendously enthusiastic and encouraging,' he said. 'She'd stir vats of boiling rubber, discuss

Hatred stirreth up strifes; but LOVE covereth all sins.

Proverbs X, 12.

James
A watercolour of the artist's
7-year-old grandson.

Hat with Bluebells
The artist's 8-year-old granddaughter Charlotte. Exhibited at the Royal Academy 1984.
Oil on canvas.

problems of air bubbles and casting and float little suggestions which I could pick up or ignore, even if it meant her taking time off from painting.

'Even when she was painting we'd chat and discuss things. That was my education in art, and it was lovely because there was no pressure as our media were different and my work wasn't affected by hers in any way.'

In 1969, Colin had a one-man exhibition in Norwich, followed two years later, by one in London and in 1973 mother and son both had their work in the Royal Academy's Summer Exhibition. Bunty's pictures were *Paper*

Boats, Agates and Cornelians and *Henry.* Colin's small brass sculpture was of his wife lying in the bath. The previous year he married a girl he had known for some time and Bunty painted *Diana,* a romantic profile of her daughter-in-law with her swirling hair caught up in a bow and a sewing needle in her mouth.

With portraits, her joy in painting continued to be more apparent in family pictures than in the constraint of commissioned ones.

'To be commissioned to paint someone's portrait is like giving a pint of blood,' she said. 'It can be very trying.

They always want to be flattered. Really, the most relaxing things to paint are still life objects because they don't fidget like people, or die on you like flowers. And if they get dusty you just blow on them.'

Three years later mother and son again showed in the Academy. Bunty's romantic little oils were in marked contrast to Colin's exhibit. He was, by then, living in Greece with his wife and two children, and had an ambitious representation in brass and bronze of the mythological Greek figures *Orpheus and Eurydice.* Afterwards, in parallel to Bunty's early successes, his work was accepted by the London Society of Portrait Sculpture and the Paris Salon. He also had one-man exhibitions in London, Amsterdam and Athens.

His carvings, in translucent white marble or olive wood, were the epitome of sensuality. Some were abstract shapes suggested by the materials themselves, others were specifically related to the human body. Creation, the recurrent life-force, was always his basic theme. His work reflected, in the beauty of local materials, the loveliness and femininity of the island of Paros in the Cyclades where he had built his marble and stone house overlooking the sea and planted an olive grove.

Although mother and son were again geographically apart their relationship had never been closer. But he saw her through the eyes of a young artist as

REMBRANDT (1606-1669)
Grijsaard met lange baard. Ets, ca. 1630
Old man with a flowing beard. Etching, ca. 1630

For Sunday 20th.
I am making it
Mother-in-law
Sunday, as you
are the most loving
special and best
Mum-in-law in the
world all my most
fondest love your adoring
Everything is perfect
here. XX Diana xx

Coll. Museum 'Het Rembrandthuis', Amsterdam

B. 291-76

Mrs. J. Miller
Broad Cottage
Surlingham
NORWICH
NORFOLK
ENGLAND.

The above - one of my most precious messages.

well as a son.

'My main quarrel with her was that she never painted enough,' he said. 'She allowed so many people to waste her time. She tried to do something for every person with whom she came in contact. She helped them, listened to their problems, wrote endless letters. She'd go to unbelievable lengths to make things for people, find just the right cards and gifts and right wrapping paper. She was loved for that and she thrived on that sort of admiration. It was lovely and very commendable but, apart from the cost, she spent so much time doing all this when I felt she should have been painting.'

The incessant present-giving, almost amounting to a compulsion, may have sprung from a subconscious need to secure the great affection and admiration her beauty and personality had always engendered.

'It's only from an artistic point of view that I criticise her,' Colin said, 'because she was a simply wonderful mother. But I thought it was criminal that someone with such talent was not painting more. She told me about her wonderful ideas and she did one or two lovely looser paintings – much freer and lighter and more open in style – but she never signed them. She'd have adored to break out and paint reflections and lights

Mollusc
A carving in olive wood by Colin Miller.
Exhibited at the Alpine Club, London 1989.

Marbles
Exhibited at the Royal Academy 1986.
Oil on panel.

coming through windows and the patterns they created. She should have pushed herself to the limit and used her talent to paint lots of different things, but her great need to do things for other people and please them interfered.

'She'd painted in the same style for nearly thirty years and felt that, artistically, she was in a rut, but she didn't have the guts to change. She couldn't handle the idea of not being accepted by the R.A. I told her she'd

Bunty Miller 1986

Bunty Miller 1979.

Butterfly
This painting shows the influence of Andrew Wyeth. Exhibited at the Royal Academy 1979.
Oil on panel.

nothing to lose by sending in two in her usual style and one quite different. Those small still lifes took so much more out of her than a freer type of painting would have. I don't know whether she felt confident enough to do it but I was confident she could. She could have turned her hand to anything.'

Colin's criticism was perhaps endorsed by Bunty's tremendous admiration for her American contemporary, Andrew Wyeth, and his evocative painting of the obvious and the commonplace, full of emotional overtones. She longed to paint in tempera, as he did, grinding the pigments into powders, mixing them with watered egg yolk and applying with fine water-colour brushes. But, sadly, she never found the time to try out the slow, patient, detailed technique by which, Wyeth said, he 'felt he could paint the air within the shadow of a blue jacket.'

I share his love for old tattered faded precious things, Bunty wrote to Undine.'*May you share my love for him.'*

Moved by the charm of pictures

which gave tantalising glimpses through window panes shrouded in flimsy curtains, she painted a butterfly fluttering against a lightly-curtained window. But not in tempera, for she had no time to experiment.

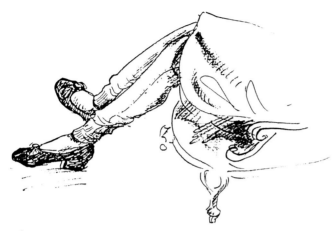

Mum was very cold - as she oft en was lately poor darling, & so this particular Easter I lent her Jimmy's shooting Longjohns! Such a glorious sense of humour had she - & was such a good SPORT she didn't in the least mind my doing this quick scribble - (O how I BLESS her several times EVERYDAY of my life ... June 12th 1985) "Clickety Click" Yesterday!!

Instead, she busied herself with helping a neighbour, Caroline Agar, to compile a book of photographs called *Pebbles and Pearls*. Bunty found old brooches and borrowed her friends' jewellery for the illustrations and made tiny decorative flower-like arrangements of polished pebbles and cornelians. Afterwards, she polished hundreds of pebbles from the Norfolk beaches and found imaginative containers for them to give as presents to her friends. More and more such distractions intruded on her painting.

Her sister Pamela died after a nine-month illness and, during that time, Bunty hardly left her side. From then on, her devotion to her widowed mother dominated her life. There were frequent visits to her elegant little flat in Norwich, long daily telephone calls and Bunty took her to all the social occasions which interested her.

There were many, for Enid retained her good looks and remained lively and elegant until the end of her life. She was an impressive figure, usually dressed in mauve, which, she claimed, was her colour, and with never a hair out of place. Uncharacteristically for a painter, Bunty followed her example and never went out without completing an elaborate toilet.

'I'd never seen such a close mother-daughter relationship in my life,' Jimmy said. 'They absolutely adored each other. Both were incredibly generous but Bunty's generosity was out of all bounds. She couldn't help it although I kept telling her we just couldn't afford it.'

For Bunty, occasional visits to Paros with Jimmy were the highlights of the year. She loved the casual life and the warmth and beauty. She sketched flowers in water-colour and did a portrait of her grandson, James, which, in due course, would be followed by a bewitching study of her nine-year-old granddaughter, Charlotte, shown in the 1984 Royal Academy as *Hat with Bluebells*. She never found time to paint comparable portraits of Undine's sons, Nicholas and Charles because they lived in London and she saw less of them.

On Jimmy's retirement in 1979, he and Bunty had moved to a small, more convenient Georgian house near the centre of Norwich. It had needed extensive renovations and, while they were being carried out and garages and sheds at the end of the garden converted to a studio, Enid Pearson was taken seriously ill. They moved into her small flat where Bunty painted in the dining-room and was by her side until she died in 1981. For four years, around that time, there were only two Bunty Miller paintings each year in the Royal Academy.

Sometime after Enid's death the author, M. M. Kaye, a fan of Bunty's work who had never managed to buy a picture, received a letter from Bunty to say she had a small painting called *Letters* which she thought the author might like to buy. The letters in the picture had been written by Enid in 1915 to her future husband, and Bunty had found them in a locked box after her death. She enclosed a snap-shot of the painting.

'Pinned to the letter,' Mollie Kaye remembered, 'was a single pressed violet. Goff, my husband, tried to remove the pin, only to find it wasn't real. The pin and the violet were a small exquisite piece of *trompe l'œil*.'

She described how, since 1957, the centenary year of the Indian Mutiny, Enid Pearson had been her most faithful fan. In that year M. M. Kaye published her first historical novel, *Shadow of the Moon,* which became an instant best seller. She had already written children's books and thrillers and there would be other books set in India, notably *The Far Pavilions,* but always, *Shadow of the Moon,* she said, had remained her firm favourite. It drew more fan letters than

> *Hast thou a friend?
> Says an Eastern Proverb
> Visit him often, for thorns
> and brushwood obstruct
> the path which no one treads.

> This was told to me by
> Jimmy's mother — & I have
> treasured it ever since.

all her other books put together.

Among the first was a wildly enthusiastic one written in an assortment of different coloured inks and lavishly decorated with gold and silver, from Enid Pearson.

'It was such a captivating letter,' its recipient recalled, 'that I replied to it at some length, whereupon I immediately received another, equally decorative and exclamatory, urging me to get the book filmed at all costs and enclosing a complete list of the actors and actresses the writer considered should play the various characters. Only the very best would do, and the all-star cast she suggested would have put *Gone with the Wind* in the shade. For instance, Laurence Olivier, who was then the reigning matinée idol of the day, was down to play a mere walking on role.

'Enid Pearson obviously had very large ideas and *Shadow of the Moon* seemed to have become her bible. She apparently read it three or four times a year and wrote numerous letters to me, usually to alter the casting because the original actors she had suggested were getting too old for the parts. Her letters were always beautifully decorated.

'I thought she was a little crazy until, with amazing perception, at one stage, she suggested that Audrey Hepburn should play the part of the heroine, Winter. When I was writing the book I'd based Winter's appearance on the photo of an unknown girl in a cold cream advert and, several years later, the girl in the photo became famous as Audrey Hepburn.'

Over the years Enid Pearson wrote hundreds of letters to Mollie Kaye.

'Perhaps she was lonely,' the writer said, 'and my book made a terrific difference to her life. I think she identified with it because, like me, she had been a Raj wife and it was set in the India she knew so well.

'In time, she sent me photographs of her three beautiful daughters and a snap of herself. You could not have wished for a more glamorous quartet. Occasionally, I received a brief note saying such things as "I have seen JUST the right man to play Alex!" Often they were scribbled inside printed cards of reproductions of Bunty's paintings. Every picture was enchanting.

'Goff was no mean painter himself and became a fan of hers. Whenever we managed to visit the Academy's Summer Exhibition he would make straight for her pictures, but they were always sold.

'We met when we were visiting Norwich. Enid invited us to lunch in her charming little flat and, to our delight, Bunty was there with her husband. Goff was delighted to meet a painter he so admired and, over the years, he wrote to her complaining that he could never make the Private View Day at the Academy in time to buy one of her pictures.'

Major-General Goff Hamilton, on seeing Bunty's letter to his wife, wrote back saying he would be delighted to buy the painting *Letters* for his wife's birthday present and Bunty ensured that, when it hung in the 1985 Royal Academy, it was his painting.

It was one of Mollie Kaye's most prized possessions.

'It's a bit of old India,' she said. 'We all used to write letters like that with stamps like that. The worst part of having an Empire was the separation of husbands and wives, parents and children. All the horror of separation is represented by those letters, tied up with a sentimental satin ribbon.'

By offering Mollie Kaye the picture – or perhaps even painting it with her in mind – Bunty could have found no better way of thanking her for the years of pleasure she had given her mother by indulging Enid Pearson's love of letter-writing and enabling her to play with her dreams of the theatre until the end of her life.

When distances divide there is no more rewarding relationship than a letter-writing one ...

Letters, India, 1915
'... a bit of old India ... representing all the horror of separation,'
(M. M. Kaye).
Exhibited at the Royal Academy 1985.
Oil on panel.

In 1982, to Bunty's joy, Colin returned with his family to England because of the children's education and made a permanent home in Norfolk, returning to Paros for a few months each year. So Bunty watched him – and often advised him – as he worked on his first Norwich landmark, *Wader,* a large bronze of a graceful woman, her skirts hoisted, her shoes dangling from her hand, destined for the riverside gardens of a hotel.

It was followed by two life-sized bronzes *Adam and Eve,* commissioned by an international food company for their London headquarters. He sculpted a young naked couple, touchingly vulnerable, languidly perched on a wall, their legs dangling, in a modern concept of the world-old problem.

Most ambitious was a group of five bronze figures also destined to become a Norwich landmark; *Gaea,* an eight-foot-high statue named after the mythological Greek goddess, portrayed a mother cradling her children in representation of the security and protection offered by the insurance company who had commissioned it. In 1990, it was unveiled by the Duke of Gloucester. Two years previously, Bunty's maternal pride had also been confirmed when her son-in-law, Mark Potter, was made a High Court Judge and received a knighthood.

By then, it was apparent that painting was no longer Bunty's prime purpose in life if, fundamentally, it ever had been. Perhaps, for someone born in June,

under the sign of Gemini, a mixture of the earthly and the heavenly twins, the dual pull of an artistic career and a practical caring mission to help others was insoluble. Her conflict epitomised the eternal female dilemma of a career versus domesticity.

'It had got to the stage when she was painting only once a year,' Colin said. 'Come January and February she couldn't be disturbed while she was painting her three pictures for the Academy. I wouldn't have argued if it was something that had gone on all through the year, but it hadn't ... '

There was one exception to Colin's assertion that she was painting pictures only for the Academy. In 1986 Bunty tackled a commission which gave full scope for her eye for detail and her talent for portraying in charismatic pictures tiny objects with minute accuracy. Once she would have revelled in the invitation, but she seemed unwell and worked so slowly and intermittently that it took her eighteen months to paint the picture.

The painting was commissioned by Lord Brownlow as a fiftieth birthday present for his wife. Lord Brownlow was the last owner of Belton House in Lincolnshire which had been his family's home for twelve generations. He had inherited it from his father, Peregrine, a close supporter of King Edward VIII during the abdication crisis, a friendship suggested by an evocative pastel by Frank Salisbury, among the Brownlow's collection of portraits, showing the young King in military uniform.

Edward, as Prince of Wales, had often stayed at Belton and was godfather to the present Lord Brownlow who, six years after his father's death, had given Belton to the National Trust. He moved to Jersey where he met Bunty and invited her to paint a picture showing a collection of his wife's most cherished souvenirs.

Bunty arranged them on a table. There was a tiny posy vase holding Shirley Brownlow's favourite spring flowers, a little wooden shoe her husband had given her on their tenth wedding anniversary, a gold bee he had given her on the birth of their son and a locket containing a jewel mounted on a scrap of material woven from the hair of the Duke of Wellington. Seemingly it had been given by the Iron Duke to one of his lady loves. There was also an Egyptian scarab and a string of beads from Thailand – both holiday souvenirs.

All were displayed on a patchwork quilt worked more than a century ago by Lady Marian Alford, Lord Brownlow's ancestor who, in 1872, was the first Vice-President of the Royal School of Needlework when Queen Victoria's third daughter, Helena, was President.

Lady Marian was an art historian as well as a needlewoman and her great tome, *Needlework as Art*, dedicated to Queen Victoria, became required reading for students of the history of interior and personal design.

I have found, she wrote in it, *so much amusement in learning for myself the history of the art of embroidery and in tracing the beginnings and the interchange of national schools that I cannot but hope that I may excite a similar interest in some of my readers and so induce those who are capable to help and lift it to a higher place than it has been allowed in these latter days to occupy.*

Lady Alford would have delighted in Bunty's portrayal of her work, with her quilt arranged so that pride of place was given to a little appliqued heart. It was Bunty Miller's last commissioned painting.

*But true love is a durable fire
In the mind ever burning;
Never sick, never old, never dead,
From itself never turning.*

Sir Walter Raleigh.

After it was finished, Jimmy and Bunty went on a long-promised nostalgic holiday to India. Mark and Undine were with them for the first stage of the journey and saw the Taj Mahal and visited Jaipur and Udaipur. Then Jimmy and Bunty went on alone to Mount Abu where they had met and married nearly half a century ago.

It was a discouraging trip and there were several minor annoyances including poor service and disappointing accommodation, and Jimmy was sorry they had ever returned to the country

they had both loved. On the way back to Jaipur he saw lines of Indian women carrying stones for road building on their heads in the full heat of the day, and he felt an illogical misgiving when he compared those pre-maturely old women to his beautiful wife.

Again he felt irrationally uncomfortable when Bunty invited a local woman to their hotel to demonstrate to her the art of Mehndi, the pre-marital Hindu ritual of decorating the hands and feet of the bride and friends and relatives with

A collection of cherished souvenirs - the artist's last commissioned painting.
1986.
Oil on panel.

MARRIAGE ∞

This day is almost done. When the night and morning meet it will only be an unalterable memory. So let no unkind word, no careless doubting thought, no guilty secret, no neglected duty, no whisp of jealous fog becloud its passing.

Now, in token of our deep and abiding love, we would lay aside all disturbing thoughts, all misunderstandings, all unworthiness. If things have gone awry, let neither of us lift an accusing finger. Who is to blame is not important; only how we shall set the situation right. And so, serving and being served, loving and being loved, we shall make a peaceful home, where we and our children shall learn to face life joyfully, triumphantly, so near as God shall give us grace.

intricate floral patterns in green paint made from henna. She covered Bunty's palm with an example of the art. Slowly, the green turned to bright orange which, over the weeks, gradually faded. Before it did so Bunty's and Jimmy's lives had been irrevocably shattered.

The day after the demonstration they went to a birthday party given by the Maharajah of Jaipur, who had been a guest at their wedding, for his eighteen-year-old daughter, an aspiring artist.

They arrived at the Palace with their presents of artist's materials and art books which Bunty carried up to the Zenana, the reception hall where only the women were allowed. Walking along the red carpet she either caught her heel or became dizzy, tripped and fell hard against a marble-topped table. When Jimmy got to her she was lying on the floor with a badly broken arm.

Surgeons at the local hospital tried to manipulate it but the pain remained unendurable. They caught the next plane to England and, when the swelling in the arm subsided, Bunty was operated on in a London hospital. Four months later she had an operation to remove the wires from her arm. It was her left arm but she never painted again.

Nine months afterwards, in November 1988, Bunty had another operation. It was for breast cancer, but by Christmas she was well enough to enjoy the family party at Adrian's North Norfolk home. In the Spring, to complete her convalescence, Jimmy and she went to the Dordogne to stay with an author friend, Christopher Wood. He was an amusing companion who, under the name of Timothy Lea, had written a series of fictional autobiographies starting with *Confessions of a Window Cleaner*.

He had restored an old stone house in the pretty village of Collonges la Rouge where, at the start of that long hot summer, there was no better place for Bunty to regain her strength. She and Jimmy strolled in the woods, went for short walks and drove to see the nearby châteaux. But within two weeks Bunty had grown so weak that, on the journey home, she needed a wheelchair to get to and from the plane.

Back at home she seemed to improve slightly and, on 11th June, they held a small party there for family and a few close friends to celebrate Bunty's seventieth birthday. There was tea in the small garden where the clusters of white roses and white geraniums were starkly beautiful against the banks of dark green shrubs. Bunty looked serene and lovely, and few guests knew of the tremendous effort she had taken with her appearance and the difficulty she had had in negotiating the flight of stairs from her bedroom. Within days a specialist confirmed that the cancer had spread uncontrollably.

During the following weeks Jimmy or Colin hardly left her side. She died at home on 12th August and was buried under a yew tree in the little graveyard at Surlingham Church, near the house where she had loved and painted for twenty years.

Until her last days her preoccupation for caring for others persisted. When Mary Colman hurt her leg she received a postcard from Bunty written in large shaky handwriting with brown ink saying:

I am so deeply distressed, my poor darling. My most tender thoughts and love always. Remember only the Happy Hours. B.

Bunty Miller herself will be long remembered. Hundreds of vibrant romantic pictures which, once acquired, no purchaser has ever been known to sell, testify to the amazing talent of a self-taught painter whose upbringing and circumstances and, above all, her generosity of spirit and her need to give and receive love, could well have deprived her of the selfish attitude to life which enables the great painters to dedicate themselves completely to their art.

Nevertheless, the artistic talent she inherited, whether or not she was able to extend it to its potential, was developed and passed on to her sculptor son and, conceivably, to his son James. If indeed James, already an art student, proves to be the sixth generation custodian of that talent he will be the first to lay firm foundations for developing it by studying at a recognised establishment.

Meanwhile, the love Bunty gave and engendered, at whatever cost to her painting, is signified by a sturdy little whitebeam flourishing in the north of Scotland, planted in her memory in the grounds of her nephew Adrian's northern home, and by a heart which Colin carved on her simple gravestone.

LOVE

LOVE is your last chance. There is really nothing else on earth to keep you there.

PAINTINGS EXHIBITED AT THE ROYAL ACADEMY

1959 Still life: Red Taffeta Rose
1960 Still life: the Last of Miranda
      Still life: Organdy Rose
      Windfalls
1961 Still life: New Rose
      Still life: Ribbons
1962 Still life: Red Silk Shoes
      Still life: Spring Headdress
1963 Coral Plume
      Still life: Bouquet
      Camelia
1964 Stephanotis
      Flowers and Fruit
      Pink Silk Shoes
1965 Red Pocket Handkerchief
      Still life: Jockey Cap
      Still life: Hat
1966 Still life: Violets
      Barrister's Wig
1967 Polyanthus
      Summer Garland
1968 Head in Moat House Wood
      Snowdrops

1969 Parcel of Flowers
      Polished Stones
      Pebbles
1970 Egg Collection
      Spring Bunch
      Mother of Pearl
1971 Mineral Study
      Contra Ora
1972 Victoria
      Letters
1973 Paper Boats
      Agates and Cornelians
      Henry
1974 Head from Moat House
        Wood II
      Silver Flask
      Mille Fiori Vase
1975 Daisy Chain
      Pollyanna
1976 Spring Bunch
      Violets
1977 Windfalls
      Still Life
      The Old Flag

1978 Snowdrops
      Eggs from Bixley
      Summer Hat
1979 Flowers from Stanley Mill
      Butterfly
      Polyanthus II
1980 Effie's Arrival
      Violets
1981 Violets
      Bride
1982 Effie and Dominoes
      Message
1983 Violets
      Orange Blossom
1984 Love Letter
      Silk Ribbons
      Hat with Bluebells
1985 Parma Violets
      Letters, India, 1915
1986 Marbles
      Heartsease
1987 Pearls and Paper
      Pansy and Polyanthus

Paintings photographed by Charles Nicholas, Jon Nicholson, Peter Trenchard, Geay (Antibes)
except 'Daisy Chain' and 'Hat with Bluebells' reproduced by kind permission of Hanson White-Accord